Quick & Easy Flower Design

QUARRY

Quick&Easy
FlowerDesign

MORE THAN 125 COLORFUL RECIPES FOR EVERYDAY ARRANGEMENTS

JESSICA WROBEL

QUARRY BOOKS

First published in the United States of America by:
Quarry Books, a member of
Quayside Publishing Group, Inc.
33 Commercial Street
Gloucester, Massachusetts 01930-5089
Telephone: (978) 282-9590
Fax: (978) 283-2742
www.rockpub.com

Library of Congress Cataloging-in-Publication Data

Wrobel, Jessica.
    Quick and easy flower design : more than 125 colorful
  recipes for everyday arrangements / Jessica Wrobel.
        p. cm.

Includes bibliographical references.
    1. Flower arrangement. I. Title.
  SB449.W76 2005
  745.92—dc22   2004024461
                                                      CIP

ISBN-13: 978-1-59253-151-6
ISBN-10: 1-59253-151-2
10 9 8 7 6 5 4 3 2

Design: Q2A Creative
All photos by Allan Penn
except pages 98 & 99 by John Cosner

Printed in Singapore

✳ contents

chapter 5 MONOTONE RECIPES **100**

introduction

Flowers can seem to be the ultimate indulgence. Their mere presence in our lives offers us a piece of nature's decadence. Yet, despite their finery, they needn't be a burden on our budgets or our hectic schedules. A few well-placed blooms can brighten the mood of any room. A little creativity and ingenuity can allow these little touches of outdoor heaven to grace our environments year-round.

Fresh cut flowers, foliage, branches, and other botanicals offer the perfect means of enhancing our homes and workspaces. Though professional floral designers get their supplies primarily through wholesale flower markets, the home designer has access to myriad resources for beautiful materials. Florist shops, the produce section of your local grocery store, farm stands,

farmers' markets, the roadside, and even your own backyard all offer a vast array of inexpensive and inspirational elements for your own creations.

This book is divided into sections by color palette: Vibrant Designs, Cool-Tone Designs, Warm-Tone Designs, and Monotone Designs. Each chapter explains the impact of these color palettes on their surroundings and offers alternative color ideas, new combinations of materials, or novel container choices for each sample design. You will learn the proper techniques—and tricks of the trade—for working with and caring for your products. You will be pushed to look outside the typical perception of what's available to you by bringing berries, herbs, and other unusual elements into your designs.

getting started

Some of us choose our professions. Others find that their professions choose them. I fall into the latter category. I did not set out on a path toward flower design, but at the fork in the road, I was beckoned, and I allowed myself to be enticed away from my previously determined route. The winding adventures that followed taught me lessons of artistic creativity, skill, and fortitude. Now, with some years' hindsight, I realize I made the right choice.

I have a great appreciation for all things beautiful—manmade and natural. During the beginning of my professional career, when I worked with fibers and fabrics, my wonderfully creative peers exposed me to new fields, techniques, and ideas. Through accidental circumstances, I found myself immersed in a flower design studio, and I started learning the ropes. Apprenticeships and the freedom to experiment with design led me to this creative place. My mentors gave me leeway to express my own visions while fulfilling those of the clients. Over time, I established my own studio, and my own clients now allow me to create and interpret their

floral dreams. My daily commute takes me to a workplace that is full of assorted flowers, potteries, vases, tools, and supplies (and a fair amount of shriveled, discarded plant matter that insists on carpeting the studio floor). At the end of the day, beauty arises from chaos: rows of centerpieces line the cooler; lush, oversized displays are ready to deck altars; and aromatic bridal bouquets await their ribbons, anticipating their short trips down wedding aisles.

Fulfillment comes to us in many shapes and forms. Many of us are drawn to the garden, inspired by the visions we take in while hiking the mountains, fields, and seacoasts, or even in the beautiful flora in our neighbors' yards. We want to incorporate those little pieces of divinity into our daily lives.

If you're like me, it's hard to stifle the inspiration derived from the verbascum you spied on last night's walk and the seckel pears you saw recently at the grocery store. When your creativity urges you to pair these two elements in an arrangement, the fact that you are not a professional floral artist should not deter you. Witnessing the sights of your mind's eye coming to fruition and seeing the appreciation on our loved ones' faces when we share our creations with them is all that can be asked.

How to begin can, at times, seem an overwhelming task. Getting over the hurdle of your presumed abilities and skill sets (or lack thereof) can be a daunting challenge. But this avocation requires only taking the rose

by the thorns and diving in. Arm yourself with a bucket of water and the tool of your choice, and you are ready for self-expression. As you will note in the Tools section, there is a variety of means of cutting your botanical elements. Most professional designers work with a knife. I, however, am not one of them. Garden scissors and clippers are my preference—scissors for the most delicate of tasks such as trimming the ends of soft-stem flowers, and clippers for just about everything else. I am frequently mocked for the number of pairs of these indispensable tools that somehow manage to overflow my back pockets.

Most of us know the appeal of shopping ventures. On your next outing, turn the trip into an inspirational pilgrimage. While flowers themselves often send creativity into overdrive, general design notions frequently start from the bottom up, based on the color, shape, or form of a container you find. A few years back, when I moved into my home, I found exquisite vintage ceramics and glassware lining the back corners of basement shelves. They were dust-encrusted and forgotten by the elderly former resident, but new life was breathed into them by the ideas they spawned in me.

Our options need not be limited by the fortuity of a change of address, however. Every houseware store, outlet, flea market, or yard sale holds the treasures and the seeds of brilliant ideas. And that is just the start of it. An inexpensive basket can be transformed into an intricately sculpted vessel by dipping it into plaster of Paris, creating a beautiful relief affect. Rows of pearls transform a wooden box from plain to high society. Embellish a simple vase with beads or gems. Accentuate it with ribbon or jute cord. Above all, don't hesitate to fine-tune the details to suit your inner vision.

The world is laden with the horticultural blessings of Mother Nature. Thanks to world trade, "seasonal" has almost lost its relevance. When it is summer in your hometown, it is winter on the other side of the planet. The growing season has been infinitely extended, and world trade has given us access to its fruits, flowers, greens, and vegetables. That said, locally grown products are often the most inexpensive, the freshest, and the most environmentally sound option. Neighborhood farms fill numerous and ever-expanding market niches. One grower's specialty is astounding vines of clematis, while another's may be exquisite dahlias, offering blooms the size of your hand. It shouldn't be too hard to find your own local resources.

My dog and I frequently take walks in our little corner of the world. We take to the woods, fields, beaches, or riverfronts as whim strikes. Wild blueberry, tender new fern shoots, hearty rosa rugosa, and sea grasses titillate with their promise for design satisfaction. My canine companion reveals secret troves to me, her head deeply burrowed into a thicket. I coax her back into daylight to delight in the low-growing berries she's discovered in the overgrowth. They will make the perfect boutonniere or create a wonderful pairing with the hollyhock from the garden.

What we can't find we can grow ourselves. We are limited, of course, by the climate, space, and amounts of sunlight and precipitation in the areas in which we live. Despite my ability to keep a cut flower looking fresh for weeks on end, gardening does not come easily to me. Nonetheless, hosta is my forte, and I delight in being able to include my favorite variegated leaves as the framework for a nosegay. The herbs from the raised beds in the backyard await their task of either garnishing the dinner salad or the table's centerpiece. Whatever your growing conditions, you are likely able to eke out at least some small addition to your flower artistry. Small container gardens on the patio, rugged houseplants, woodland shade gardens, or prolific perennial gardens all give their hearts and souls to the beckonings of our artistic bents. Make use of these offerings and follow the sights of your mind's eye, for this is an exquisite path to walk.

Jessica Wrobel

Tools

Artists and craftspeople know that the quality of their workmanship starts with proper preparation. Being armed with the right tools is invaluable. The floral designer's tool bag should include the following:

A STEM TAPE

B GARDEN SCISSORS

C WIRE CUTTERS

D HOT-GLUE GUN

E FABRIC AND RIBBON SCISSORS

F BRANCH CLIPPERS

G KNIFE

H FLORAL FOAM

I MOSS (left, sheet; right, sphagnum)

J WATER TUBES

K COATED WIRE

L WOODEN PICKS

M PIPE CLEANERS

N ASSORTED-GAUGE WIRE

O WATERPROOF TAPE

Not Shown ✻

BUCKETS OF VARIOUS SIZES

TOWELS AND RAGS

WATERING CANS

BLEACH

FLOWER FOOD

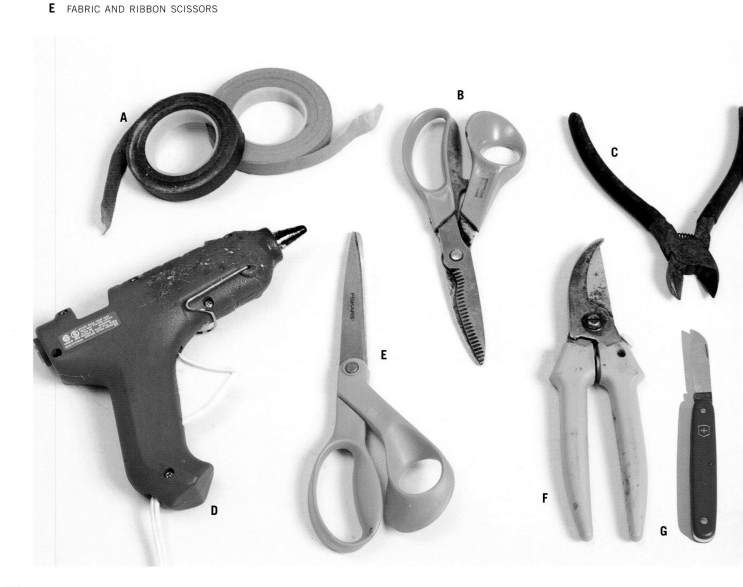

All these items are readily available at most craft or garden centers. Proper care of your flowers and greens will ensure longevity. Before you start working with your materials, regardless of where they come from, they need to be hydrated and nourished. The biggest threats to cut flowers and greens are bacteria, mold, and fungus. To eliminate this risk, rinse every bucket, vase, or other container with a diluted bleach and water solution prior to use. Fill the buckets with water, remove any leaves that will be below the water line, recut the bottom inch of the stems, and let the flowers or greens stand in the water for at least an hour before using them.

tip Roses should be cut under water to avoid trapping air bubbles in the stems, which causes the heads to droop.

Preparing Your Containers

Glass containers, which allow the stems of an arrangement to be seen, dictate that the bouquet be designed in water, not floral foam. A vase with a large opening can be difficult to arrange in. To make this process easier, use the following steps, as needed, depending on your design choice:

ABOVE If glass containers are your preference, there are many options beyond the standard vase. Bottles, in particular, come in a variety of interesting sizes and shapes.

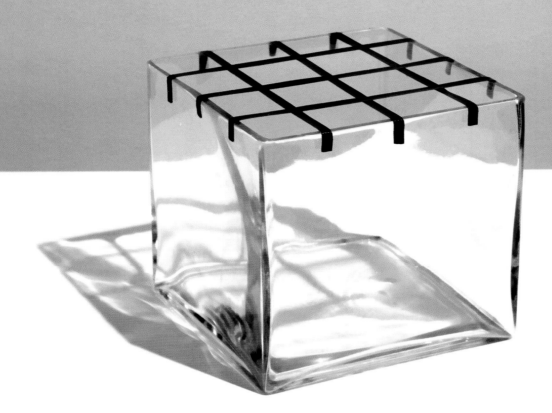

* Use waterproof floral tape to form a grid over the container's opening. This will allow you to arrange vertical elements without them falling to one side or the other

* A "frog"—a heavy, metal-spiked item, available at most craft or garden design stores—can also be used. A frog offers a visually pleasing grid that is integral to the overall design.

* You can use anything from bundled branches to small seashells or colored marbles to stabilize an arrangement. These elements add texture, color, and provide support for the stems you are working with as the design progresses.

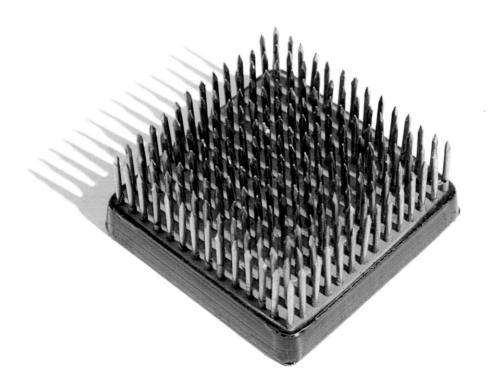

design tips and ideas
for opaque containers

✳ When working with floral foam and soft-stem flowers, such as daffodils, first make a hole in the foam with a stick of similar diameter to the stem. Inserting the stem in this premade hole will help avoid breaking, bending, or damaging the stalk.

✳ Hollow-stem flowers, such as sweet peas or delphiniums, can be further manipulated by slipping a piece of wire into the stalk. This will allow you to gently bend the stem in the direction needed or to repair a bent one. Working with a foundation of floral foam in the container further strengthens the mechanics of this technique.

TOP Basic ceramic containers come in a wide range of shapes, colors, patterns, and styles. They are easy to find at a variety of stores, yard sales, and garden centers.
LEFT Teacups, sake cups, and streamlined pitchers offer an Asian element, influencing the patterns and color palette of the design.

ABOVE A variety of rich- and warm-tone containers represent a number of different materials from ceramic to twigs to faded coppers.

RIGHT The French country look is still very popular. A wide range of containers that suit this design style is available at houseware and craft stores.

Opaque vessels such as ceramic pots, window boxes, compotes, or bowls—especially those with wide openings—generally require that the design be done in floral foam.

1 Fill a large bucket with water and drop in a block of floral foam. Allow the foam to become fully saturated before proceeding.

2 Cut the foam to fit firmly inside the container, extending about 3/4" (2 cm) above the top edge. Use the floral tape to secure it in place. Top off the container with water.

3 Moisten a piece of sheet moss, then gently pull at the edges so its structure loosens, making it easier to penetrate with the flower stems. Lay the moss over the foam—this provides coverage that will beautifully disguise the mechanics of the foam, which might be revealed by any thin spots in the final design.

ABOVE Silver adds elegance to any design, no matter what materials are used. Scavenged from flea markets or purchased new, they make a great addition to your container collection.

✳ Cutting your own flowers from the yard or roadside guarantees freshness. For best results, cut the flowers in the cool hours of the early morning or late evening, and immediately place them into a bucket of water. If you need to make up the arrangements immediately, design them in fresh water rather than in floral foam.

✳ Tulips continue to grow even after they are cut, causing them to arc,

bend, and dance into new forms even after you've arranged them. Take advantage of this endearing characteristic by using tulips in graceful freeform designs, rather than forcing them into tight, structured pieces. Given this independent streak, tulips tend to be best displayed in vases rather than in potteries that require floral foam, so that their natural tendencies are not restricted.

tip Before starting any arrangement, always top off the vase or container with water. This ensures all components of the arrangement will stay fresh.

* If a rose's head has drooped, recut the bottom of the stem under water, and let it stand until it straightens. To further assist in releasing the air bubble that has caused the drooping, use a pin to poke a small hole through the top of the stem, just below the head of the flower.

* It is a myth that an open rose does not last as long as a tight bud. Some rose varieties open very quickly into a big beautiful flower and last a while. By removing the outer petals of a rose and blowing into the center of the bloom, you can encourage faster opening. These outer petals are a natural protection for the beautiful blossom that waits within.

* Sappy flowers, such as spurge, tweedia, and daffodils, can wither as they lose their sap after a fresh cut. To prevent this, seal a freshly cut stem by holding the end over a candle flame until the seepage stops.

* Flowers don't necessarily open on our timetables, but some can be encouraged to bloom more quickly. All flowers will respond to warm water and sunlight, which makes them mature in less time. To slow down the opening of petals, keep blossoms in a cool, dimly lit area, away from drafts.

* An iris can be tickled open by gently flicking a finger at the base of the flower head. Lilies can be eased open by rolling the bloom gently between your palms. Once the bud is open, carefully cut the stamens from the inside of the flower to prevent the pollen from staining the delicate petals.

a rose by any
other name...

COMMON/ENGLISH NAME	BOTANICAL NAME
African lily, lily of the Nile	*Agapanthus africanus*
ajuga	*Ajuga reptans*
allium	*Allium* spp.
anemone	*Anemone* spp.
ageratum	*Ageratum* hybrids
astilbe	*Astilbe* spp.
bearberry, kinnikinnick	*Arctostaphyllus uva-ursi*
bamboo	*Bambusa spp.*
basil	*Ocimum basilicum*
bee balm	*Monarda didyma*
black-eyed Susan	*Rudbeckia hirta*
bleeding heart	*Dicentra formosa*
bluedick	*Dichelostemma volubile*
calathea leaf	*Calathea picturata*
calendula	*Calendula officinalis*
candytuft	*Iberis umbellata, Brassicaceae*
chamomile	*Chamaemelum nobile*
cherry blossom	*Prunus* spp.
chives	*Allium schoenoprasum*
clematis, virgin-bower	*Clematis* spp., hybrids
coleus, menthol plant	*Solenostemon scutellarioides*
columbine	*Aquilegia* spp., hybrids
coreopsis, tickseed	*Coreopsis lanceolata*
cosmos	*Cosmos atrosanguineus*
crocosmia	*Crocosmia x crocosmiiflora*

COMMON/ENGLISH NAME	BOTANICAL NAME
curly willow	*Salix matsudana*
daffodil	*Narcissus*
dahlia	*Dahlia* spp., hybrids
delphinium, larkspur	*Delphinium* spp., hybrids
dill	*Anethum graveoleus*
dock, curled dock	*Rumex crispus*
Dordogne	*Dordogne*
dusty miller	*Senecio cineraria*
English daisy	*Bellis perennis*
fiddleheads	fiddleheads
fox tail lily	*Eremurus*
freesia	*Freesia* hybrids
fuchsia	*Fuchsia* hybrids
geranium	*Pelargonium* hybrids
grape hyacinth	*Muscari armeniacum*
green bird flower	*Crotalaria cunninghamii*
hair allium	*Allium sphaerochephalon*
hens and chicks	*Echeveria* spp.
hosta, plantain lily, funkia	*Hosta* hybrids
hyacinth	*Hyacinthus orientalis*
hydrangea	*Hydrangea* spp., hybrids
hypericum	*Hypericum androsaemon*
iris	*Iris* spp., hybrids
ivy	*Hedera helix*
jonquil	*Narcissus jonquilla*
ladies' mantle	*Alchemilla mollis*

Flowers have long been a source of mystery and enticement; their origins are obscured by centuries, myths, and presumptions. The names mothers and grandmothers have assigned to blooms usually have been more than enough. These titles have become our individual histories; folk legends somehow always manage to defy botanic and etymological law. Nonetheless, the chart below translates some of our favorite flowers into dependably common language for discussing the topic. Go ahead and cross-reference, but don't forget what mother taught you.

COMMON/ENGLISH NAME	BOTANICAL NAME	COMMON/ENGLISH NAME	BOTANICAL NAME
lamb's ear, betony, bunnies' ear, hedge nettle, lamb's tongue, woundwort	*Stachys Byzantium*	pussy willow	*Salix discolor*
		Queen Anne's lace, wild carrot	*Daucus carota*
lavender	*Lavandula angustifolia*	quince	*Chaenomeles japonica* var. *alpina*
lepto bloom, tea bush	*Leptospermum scoparium*	ranunculus	*Ranunculus* spp.
lilac	*Syringa vulgaris*	rose	*Rosa* spp.
lily	*Lilium* spp., hybrids	rosemary	*Rosmarinus officinalis*
lisianthus	*Eustoma grandiflorum*	safflower	*Carthamus tinctorius*
lysimachia, loosestrife	*Lysimachia clethroides*	sage	*Salvia* spp.
maidenhair fern	*Adiantum* spp.	St. John's wort	*Hypericum perforatum*
masterwort	*Astrantia major*	scabiosa	*Scabiosa atropurpurea*
millet	*Panicum decompositum*	schefflera	*Schefflera arboricola*
million bells	*Calibrachoa* hybrids	snapdragon	*Antirrhinum majus*
mint	*Mentha* spp.	Solomon's seal	*Polygonatum multiflorum*
monkshood, helmet flower	*Aconitum napellus*	spurge	*Euphorbia* spp.
		star of Bethlehem	*Ornithogalum umbellatum*
moss, sheet moss, reindeer moss, sphagnum moss	*Sphagnum cymbifolium*	stonecrop	*Sedum* spp.
		sugar pea	*Pisum sativum* var. *macrocarpon*
Guernsey lily	*Nerine bowdenii*	sweet pea	*Lathyrus odoratus*
nigella, love-in-a-mist	*Damascena*	thistle, sea holly	*Erygnium planum*
night-blooming jessamin	*Cestrum nocturnum*	ti plant leaf	*Cordyline terminalis*
orchid	*Orchis* spp., hybrids	tulip	*Tulipia* spp.
oregano	*Origanum vulgare*	tweedia, Southern star	*Oxypetalum caeruleum, tweedia caerulea*
pansy	*Viola tricolor*		
peony	*Paeonia officinalis*	veronica, speedwell	*Veronica spicata*
peruvian lily	*Alstroemeria*	viburnum, guelder rose	*Viburnum opulus*
phlox	*Phlox* spp.	violas, johnny-jump-ups	*Viola cornuta*
poppy	*Papaver* spp.	wild or false indigo	*Baptisia australis*
		yarrow	*Achillea millefolium*

more design techniques

Most of the designs in this book are simple arrangements made directly in the vessels that contain them. But design options can expand by using many of the same flower and color combinations in different ways.

topiaries

A topiary is any kind of tightly defined shape, including spirals, globes, and cones. The shape that is most commonly identified with the term is a globe resting atop a trunk. Beyond the basic tools and supplies needed for most arranging, you will also need: chicken wire, plaster of Paris, a staple gun, and something to serve as the trunk for the arrangement. A birch branch, curly willow branches, or bundled grasses work well. As long as the trunk you choose can provide enough strength to support the head, the options are limitless.

1 Cut the trunk material to a length that will suit the proportions of the container. If you are using bundled materials, make sure that the column is tightly tied off at the top and the bottom. If you need to add strength to gathered grasses, for example, wrap them around a dowel that will be hidden in the final design.

2 Prepare the plaster of Paris as directed, then fill the container about two-thirds full. Place the trunk in the center of the container, and hold it stable while the plaster sets. Allow it to dry thoroughly before continuing.

3 Cut a piece of chicken wire slightly longer than the circumference of the intended ball shape of the topiary. Staple the wire to the trunk, low enough so that it can completely surround the floral foam ball.

4 Soak the ball of floral foam in water, and then push it down onto the trunk. Wrap the chicken wire up and over the foam to hold it in place. Secure both ends of the chicken wire together with a piece of wire.

5 Start the design by defining the shape with the larger flowers you are working with, filling in and finishing off with the smaller elements.

6 Cover the plaster around the bottom of the trunk with moss. If you'd like to include flowers in the bottom portion, simply layer some water-saturated floral foam beneath the moss to hold the blooms. Or slip flowers into water tubes that are hidden under the mossy surface.

 tip Given that there is no reservoir to hold water for the head of the topiary, the floral foam must be watered and moistened often for a long-lasting arrangement. Some flowers are better suited than others for this type of arrangement. Keep in mind that flowers with sturdy stems tend to fare better and will be easier for you to work with.

garlands

Garlands are an absolute treat. They are often used to decorate for the most special occasions, guests of honor, and the best features of homes or work places. These pieces are usually reserved for just a few special areas, as their assembly can be time consuming. With a little know-how, you'll quickly master this decorating triumph.

Garlands can be extraordinarily simple to create, if you start with the right material. Select a vine to work with, such as ivy, clematis, fresh grapevine, or vinca, to provide a natural length for the garland.

1 Wrap several lengths of ivy around each other until you have created the desired fullness. The more tendrils you add, the thicker and more lush the feel. Repeat with a second set of cuttings.

2 Line up the two sets of entwined vines, overlapping their ends by 2 to 3 inches (5 to 8 cm). Use a piece of wire to bind them together.

3 Continue in this manner until you have created the desired length of garland.

garland variation

1 Cut the blocks of floral foam widthwise into 1" (2.5 cm) squares. Cut the tulle into a strip long enough for the length of garland needed and wide enough to wrap around the foam.

2 Wrap each block of the foam you have cut with tulle, tying it off with a piece of wire. Secure each successive piece of foam in the same manner. Soak the entire length of foam and tulle in water.

3 Before inserting each of the botanical elements of your design, cut a small hole in the tulle so that the stems can pass through. Continue adding stems until the whole garland has been filled in.

For a more elaborate garland, you just need a few more easy-to-find tools and materials, including the following:

∗ floral foam

∗ strips of tulle fabric

∗ wire

∗ small fabric scissors

∗ garden scissors

Full garlands of flowers provide a romantic, lush look, but can be time consuming to make and have a fair amount of weight to them. To accomplish a similar look with less heaviness and fewer mechanics, bind small bundles of lavender, thistle, or decorative grasses to a length of twine cut to the length needed. This will provide a design that will also dry beautifully for a long-lasting keepsake.

Magenta peonies, purple sweet peas, and tangerine dahlias: a bouquet that captures the vibrancy of life in a vase. The enrapturing strands of color tell stories over the dining room table. Bedside arrangements spur us into action each day with the promise of success, and then embrace us at night with kaleidoscope dreams. What may well be the most marvelous characteristic of nature's blossoms is the multitude of magnificent jewel tones that they fashion for our pleasure.

Explosions of color enliven the weariness of winter. Make an announcement with an arrangement of lemons, oranges, fresh herbs, and raspberry-hued roses set spitefully in front of the picture window that frames the dull gray of winter weather. Summer dances with color and encourages us to revel in the celebration. Phlox, sweet peas, and garden vegetables combine for an arrangement of life's best pleasures for the taking. Vibrant tones nurture our creativity and challenge our imaginations.

refreshing cache

* **MATERIALS**
11 kumquats
raspberries
mint leaves
sage green cachepot

* **TOOLS**
branch clippers
floral foam
waterproof tape
sheet moss
wooden picks cut into
3" (8 cm) lengths

The crispness of this vibrant grouping is refreshing; it combines a symphony of colors and scents. Petite proportions make this arrangement the perfect accent for a porch or picnic table. On a larger scale, it would present a scrumptious centerpiece for a summer buffet.

1 Prepare your container with water-saturated floral foam taped in place and lightly covered with moss.

2 Use wooden picks to arrange the kumquats in the container. Add mint leaves as accents.

3 Place the raspberries in the arrangement, carefully nestling them between the greenery and the kumquats.

textural variation

Kumquats are the anchors of this piece, but the backdrop offered by the two other elements changes the feel of the design considerably. The multitude of small shapes makes this feel freestyle in form, creating a greater sense of visual movement and texture. The broader range of materials used within one arrangement, the busier and wilder it tends to feel.

✳ **BOTANICAL MATERIALS**
   kumquats
   maidenhair fern
   bearberry

styling variation

The very nature of this rustic urn changes the formality level of the arrangement. The tight and firmly formed design suggests old-world aristocracy. The nature of the materials themselves furthers the attitude of the presentation—citrus fruits are typical to this design period.

✳ **BOTANICAL MATERIALS**
   lemons
   kumquats
   pink spray roses
   green hypericum berries
   peach hypericum berries

VIBRANT : backyard elegance

* **MATERIALS**
8 lilacs
sprigs of quince
glass cylindrical vase

* **TOOLS**
branch clippers

Working with large flowering blooms, such as lilac, is surprisingly simple. They have a natural grace and movement to them and fill space quickly. Dogwood or viburnum would be wonderful substitutes for the lilac in this arrangement. To provide a different color combination, cherry blossoms or forsythia would stand in perfectly for the quince.

1 Cut the stems of lilac and arrange them in the vase, allowing the center branches to stand a bit taller than the rest. This will create a slightly domed shape.

2 Carefully insert the stems of quince between the lilac blooms.

3 Pay attention to the structure that the quince lends to the arrangement, and be careful to not overdo it.

textural variation

On a much smaller scale, this design is still eye-catching. Displaying a sparse selection of sprouted branches, the galvanized tin flower bucket is an extension of the vertical lines of the arrangement. If you would rather create a feeling of lush garden abundance, select a squat galvanized tub, and fill it with an overflowing assortment of branches.

✳ **BOTANICAL MATERIALS**
sprigs of quince
sprouted curly willow

textural variation

A wine caddy offers the same upright dimensions as the galvanized tin, but the color offers a richness that plays off the deep tones of the lilac. Moving away from the architectural feel of the stark branches, Queen Anne's lace extends beyond the boundaries of the design, further softening the effect and adding height. Decorative grasses or arching tulips could be beautiful substitutes to mimic this lovely effect.

✳ **BOTANICAL MATERIALS**
lilac
Queen Anne's lace

vibrant players

* **MATERIALS**
  10 assorted ranunculus
  2 fiddleheads
  bamboo

* **TOOLS**
  garden scissors
  coated wire
  handsaw

Bamboo is a wonderful material. At each naturally formed segment, there is a solid juncture that divides the stalk into hollow sections. Cut below these areas to create small bamboo vases. Thick pieces of bamboo can stand freely, while narrower pieces can be wrapped with ribbon, wire, or cording and hung from doorknobs, picture hangers, or curtain rods, or placed in vases with other botanicals.

1 With a small handsaw, cut the bamboo to length, and wrap the coated wire around the top, about 2" (5 cm) below the opening, to create a hanger. Add water to the hollow center of the bamboo.

2 Add the ranunculus, keeping the stems long. The contrast in height will create a sense of playfulness.

3 Cut the fiddleheads to the desired length and insert them into the arrangement.

styling variation

A natural-tone bamboo segment, wrapped with vintage ribbon, becomes the vessel for this arrangement of spray roses and ranunculus. Further decoration and embellishment could be added with antique buttons or lace. Beads and sequins would perfectly tailor the design for a formal evening affair.

✳ **BOTANICAL MATERIALS**
 ranunculus
 spray roses

styling variation

The styling here is lush and full, but still loose. Fiddleheads break away from the main body of the arrangement, adding a hint of attitude and fun to a simple glass display. In a larger glass vessel, the curled tips of the fiddleheads could be used underwater to bring the festivities down below.

✳ **BOTANICAL MATERIALS**
 ranunculus
 pink spray roses
 fiddleheads

standing tall

✳ **MATERIALS**
10 peach and orange roses
7 double flowering pink tulips
dill
5 peach hypericum
gold schefflera
curly willow

✳ **TOOLS**
garden clippers
coated wire

A freestanding bouquet is breath-taking. It is the perfect focal point for a serving or foyer table. Smaller versions are perfect complements for vanities. To add extra stability for high traffic or impact areas, fill a flowerpot saucer or serving tray with moistened sand and level your piece in it. This gives the added bonus of supplying the flowers with water for a long-lasting and eye-catching display.

1 Working in your hand, add one stem of the roses, tulips, and hypericum at a time to form a round, domed bouquet.

2 Slip stems of dill into the body of the arrangement, allowing them to stand out a bit from the other flowers. Arch branches of curly willow over the bouquet, delicately "caging" it. Tie off the bouquet with coated wire.

3 Wrap several additional branches around the wire, tucking the ends in beneath the wrapping to secure in place. Clip and adjust the stems to the desired length, making sure the bouquet will stand on a level surface.

styling variation

Cool, crisp, and airy, a stand of white dendrobium orchids wrapped with a ti leaf is the perfect accent to modern decor or a tease of paradise in a patio setting. Experiment with additional colors of orchids—from vibrant to muted—to find the complement for your space.

✳ **BOTANICAL MATERIALS**
   dendrobium orchids
   ti plant leaf

textural variation

Not only is this example visually busier with its multitude of different backyard elements, but also it offers a much more vertical styling. Its height makes it the perfect piece to enliven a forgotten corner or to create a welcoming cornerstone for your front door. When placed on porch steps, its linear shaping echoes architectural posts and beams.

✳ **BOTANICAL MATERIALS**
   lilacs
   sprigs of quince
   black and gray pussy willow
   Queen Anne's lace

cocktails at five

✳ **MATERIALS**
2 blooms of chartreuse cymbidium orchids
1 deep pink rose
martini glass

✳ **TOOLS**
garden scissors

The party begins with this delightful little number, and nothing could be easier to prepare. The rose petals not only add a splash of color, but also act as a "frog" to keep the orchids where they are placed. Even better, there is no shaking or stirring required to awaken the liveliness of this floral libation.

1 Carefully pull the petals from the rose, being sure not to tear or bruise them in the process. Use them to fill the martini glass about three-quarters full.

2 Fill the glass with water, stopping just below the rim of the glass.

3 Place one orchid bloom in the glass so that it floats on the water's surface. Perch the other over the side, making sure its stem reaches into the water.

container variation

Both the mason jar and the branches used to form the frog for this piece lend a very different feeling to the arrangement. The frog still does its job—allowing for ease of design—and holds this assortment of wildflowers perfectly in place. The very essence of the botanicals used suggests the meadow rather than high society.

✳ **BOTANICAL MATERIALS**
   columbine
   chamomile
   ladies' mantle
   scented geranium
   Queen Anne's lace
   curly willow

container variation

The earthy scents of some botanical materials, like the peppery aroma of freesia and the rich color of the coffee beans, tend to be more masculine. The whole coffee beans also provide excellent support for these blooms that offer a morning wake-up call to the senses.

✳ **BOTANICAL MATERIALS**
   freesia
   tulips
   viburnum

VIBRANT **take-out**

✳ **MATERIALS**

2 stems of bee balm
2 edible sweet peas
5 nerine lilies
2 orchids
Chinese take-out container

✳ **TOOLS**

garden scissors
floral foam
moss
small wooden pick

Everything is fun and fanfare in this delightful design of exotic shapes and colors. Take-out containers are now available in a range of sizes and colors, and they are waterproof, as well. The playfulness of this bouquet can easily be pushed to the next level with accessories. Add bundled chopsticks, paper umbrellas, or scripted good fortunes for surprise and humor, transforming a botanical package into a perfect party favor or hostess gift.

1   If the container is a remnant of last night's take out, wash it out, and then prepare it with foam and moss.

2   Start with the nerine lilies to outline the shape and size of the design. Accent with the bee balm and orchids.

3   Wire the peas to a small pick, and tuck into the bottom of the arrangement.

container variation

This bouquet has the same combination of flowers as the first. The narrower shape of the container, however, streamlines the proportions for a more delicate presentation, which is properly mimicked in the artistry of the vase.

✳ **BOTANICAL MATERIALS**
  bee balm
  nerine lilies
  orchids
  edible sweet peas

botanical variation

Weight is added to this version of the bouquet by substituting hearty red dahlias for the delicacy of the bee balm. The vivid contrast between the flowers and the container maintains excitement. Spice up the palette even further with the addition of dahlias in tones of orange and pink, or tie vibrant ribbons or brooches to the neck of the vase.

✳ **BOTANICAL MATERIALS**
  red dahlia
  nerine lilies
  bee balm

VIBRANT captured

* **MATERIALS**
  11 pansies
  2 fuchsia blooms
  glass cube vase

* **TOOLS**
  garden scissors

In the professional design studio, accidental pairings on the workbench frequently lead to inspiration. This piece originated in a simple need to find a quick and easy place to give water to the accumulation of short stems generated from a work in progress. Looking up, it was suddenly clear, that the little captured faces of the blooms had many stories to tell of their own. The unplanned arrangement was moved to center stage.

1 Fill a glass cube vase about one-third full with water. You need enough water to nourish the blooms, while still keeping the design plane below the rim of the vase.

2 Carefully arrange four or five stems of the pansies in the base of the vase, allowing them to form something of a framework to support the rest of the blooms.

3 Add the rest of the stems of pansies, keeping some faces forward, pressed against the glass. Garnish the finished arrangement with a touch more color, laying the blooms of fuchsia alongside the vase.

styling variation

The choice of flower, and its inherent personality, naturally imbues a certain level of formality. Small white roses waltz beneath the vase line, while delicate astilbes curtsy up above. Both partners are clearly in view, while coupling perfectly.

✳ **BOTANICAL MATERIALS**
   white spray roses
   pink astilbe

container variation

Different vase shapes provide a variety of options for the canvas you are working with. Some will stretch the imagination with height or width, while others contain your vision more concisely. Faintly colored glass could lend color to the design, offering something of a rose-colored spectacle to view the masterpiece through.

✳ **BOTANICAL MATERIALS**
   bee balm
   dichelostemma

VIBRANT : vines of glory

⁂ **MATERIALS**
6 green croatalaria
4 pink sweet pea vines
2 stems of safflower
green berry clippings
tall blue vase

⁂ **TOOLS**
garden scissors
branch clippers

Vines are an interesting design element because of their natural sense of movement and fluidity. They reach beyond the confines of structure, refusing to be constricted or maintained in any way. Each season has its own special blend of offerings for year-round enjoyment.

1 Use the clippings of the green berry branches to fill in the vase, creating a support system for the stems to follow.

2 Add the croatalaria, allowing the stems to bend and twine as they wish. Fill in the arrangement with the sweet pea vines.

3 Add the safflower stems for a touch of color contrast.

styling variation

Larger blooms, such as dahlias, provide a stronger visual for the eye to focus on. They naturally calm what would otherwise be a busy, textural piece. Lilies, peonies, or wisteria would serve this arrangement just as well as dahlias. Substitute autumn vines of bittersweet or the arched branches of wild summer raspberries and blackberries for an appropriate seasonal appeal.

✳ **BOTANICAL MATERIALS**
sweet pea vines
dahlias
safflower

botanical variation

Vines are enchanting without the presence of any flowers at all. A candleholder is transformed and gives lift to an assortment of tendrils and berries. A burning taper would restore some of the candleholder's original purpose and would color the textures of the foliage with a warm glow.

✳ **BOTANICAL MATERIALS**
croatalaria
viburnum berries
millet grass
grape leaf ivy

sundae

✳ **MATERIALS**
1 stem of white phalenopsis
orchid
2 stems of white
cymbidium orchid
stems of wild grass cuttings
handful of cherries
off-white weathered
pottery urn

✳ **TOOLS**
garden scissors
stem tape
wire
floral foam
waterproof tape
moss

The vibrancy of a bouquet can be manifested through the contrast of the tones. The striking difference between the snow white of these orchids and the richness of the red cherries set one another off dramatically. This contrast is further defined by the distinct shapes of the different forms of plant material.

1 Prepare the urn with the floral foam, waterproof tape, and moss. Select a stem of phalenopsis orchid and use it as the focal point of the design, allowing it to cascade over the side of the container.

2 Cut the stems of cymbidium orchids into shorter segments, and fill in the shape of the bouquet.

3 Mound cherries into the center of the bouquet. Wire two cherries together from the tips of their stems, and insert into the base of the arrangement so that they dangle over the side of the urn.

color variation

The same selection of botanical materials warms significantly with a simple change of colors. The toasty glow of the yellow orchids could also be enhanced with the use of golden or white cherries. The effect would be monochromatic, but striking.

✳ **BOTANICAL MATERIALS**
   cymbidium orchids
   red cherries

styling variation

This piece is practically designed inside out. A small, silver ring box supports the petals of a fully open, extravagantly large rose. This naturally formed bowl is filled with cherries, and everything is topped off with a single orchid bloom, exchanging places with the usual cherry on top.

✳ **BOTANICAL MATERIALS**
   1 large rose
   red cherries
   white cymbidium orchid

kissing colors

VIBRANT

✳ MATERIALS
1 stem of purple hydrangea
1 stem of peach hypericum berries
3 stems of red
3 stems of red crocosmia
silver ribbon

✳ TOOLS
garden scissors
floral foam
two pipe cleaners
wire
stem tape
knife

With no container at all, these flowers and colors are left to speak for themselves—and they have plenty to say. Kissing balls, or pomanders, can be designed in a full sphere, or just half way around so that they can be hung on walls or doors. The mechanics are relatively simple, and the result is the availability of 360 degrees of design creativity.

1 With a knife, shape the floral foam into a sphere about the size of a tennis ball. Twist the two pipe cleaners together into an x shape and wrap them around the foam. Loop a length of ribbon under the pipe cleaners and tie off. Soak the foam in water.

2 Use small snippets of hydrangea to fill the shape of the sphere. Add accents of the crocosmia and hypericum berries.

3 Wrap a length of wire with stem tape. Twist this around the center of a piece of ribbon that will serve as the streamers. Cut the wire to about 1 1/2" (4 cm), and slip it into the bottom of the foam.

botanical variation

The key to a successfully constructed kissing ball is the use of a large flower as the primary element to provide ample surface coverage, while taking up little space within the mechanics of the floral foam. This allows for both the maximum water availability per stem, and also maintains the integrity of the structure.

✳ **BOTANICAL MATERIALS**
star of Bethlehem
burgundy spray rose

color variation

Pomanders are lovely accents for doorknobs, curtain rods, and fireplaces. The colors can be rich and bold or soft and subtle. Take the backdrop into consideration when choosing your palette, and take full advantage of the materials at hand. Use the pomanders singly, or group arrangements of assorted-sized pieces for a breathtaking display.

✳ **BOTANICAL MATERIALS**
green hydrangea
bluedicks
peach hypericum berries
orange rose

gift giving

Everyone loves to receive flowers, and for the giver, the fun is in being inspired. Select your flowers, greens, and other botanical materials to reflect the tastes and preferences of the people you are giving to. Keep in mind the colors they like, how they decorate their home, even how they dress. A detail from their favorite handbag or cufflink may be the very inspiration needed to perfectly personalize the token of your affection. These are all clues on how to make the best impression with your presentation.

Lacy, miniature shapes take on new form when densely packed together, and the petite proportions of this bottled piece make it a darling gift for a small child. A very simple green grosgrain tie quietly announces this bundle of joy.

A scrap of silk or a vintage hankie adds a special touch and brings character and practicality to the presentation. Beneath the soft folds of the fabric, water tubes or damp wrappings may be concealed, assuring the freshness and beauty of the flowers.

The rich tones of the flowers and the striking copper pot provide a handsome, masculine feel for this gift. The copper name tag coordinates with the pot and reminds us of the bouquet's garden origins.

botanical expressions

Everybody understands the proclamation of love that arrives with red roses delivered on Valentine's Day. But the sentiments of a tulip or a daisy or a sprig of rosemary may not be as clear. Floriography, the meaning of flowers, has a long history, but truly only developed into its own secret language during the nineteenth century as a means to speak from the heart within the strict confines of Victorian etiquette. Proposals could be accepted or refused; inclinations and heartstrings were boldly proclaimed without the uttering of one syllable. The sentiments were bound with beautiful ribbons and offered with silent eloquence.

COMMON/ENGLISH NAME	BOTANICAL EXPRESSION	COMMON/ENGLISH NAME	BOTANICAL EXPRESSION
ANEMONE	*fragility; abandonment*	HYDRANGEA	*perseverance;understanding; frigidity; heartlessness*
APPLE BLOSSOM	*promise; preference*	IRIS	*inspiration and good health; faith; wisdom; hope; promise*
ASTILBE	*I'll be waiting*		
BASIL	*best wishes; success in love*	IVY	*fidelity; the symbol of marriage*
CANDYTUFT	*indifference*		
CHAMOMILE	*energy in action*	JONQUIL	*affection returned*
CHERRY BLOSSOM	*education*	LAVENDER	*distrust; luck*
CLEMATIS	*esteem*	LILAC	*first love*
DAFFODIL	*chivalry*	LILY	*purity*
DAISY	*innocence*	LISIANTHUS	*calming*
DAHLIA	*elegance; forever thine*	MAIDENHAIR FERN	*secret bond of love; discretion*
DELPHINIUM	*boldness; big-hearted;fun*	MINT	*virtue*
DILL	*lust*	MONKSHOOD	*beware; danger is near*
DOGWOOD	*duration*	MOSS	*maternal love; charity*
EREMURAS	*endurance*	NUTS	*stupidity*
EUPHORBIA	*persistence*	ORCHID	*delicate beauty; you are beautiful; Chinese symbol for "many children"*
FERN	*fascination*		
FREESIA	*spirited; innocence; trust*	PANSY	*loving thoughts of you; merriment*
FRITILLARIA	*majesty*		
FUCHSIA	*good taste; confiding love*	PEARS	*sweet affection*
GERANIUM	*comfort*	PEONY	*healing*
GRASS	*submission*	PHLOX	*unanimity*
HYACINTH	*sincerity; rashness*		

COMMON/ENGLISH NAME	BOTANICAL EXPRESSION
POPPY	*consolation; oblivion; eternal sleep*
PUSSY WILLOW	*motherhood*
QUEEN ANNE'S LACE	*delicate femininity*
RANUNCULUS	*radiant; I am dazzled by your charms*
ROSE	*love*
ROSEMARY	*remembrance; commitment*
SAGE	*great wisdom*
SCABIOSA	*I cannot accept your love*
SNAPDRAGON	*presumptuous; no*
STAR OF BETHLEHEM	*atonement; reconciliation*
SUNFLOWER	*adoration*
SWEET PEA	*shyness; lasting pleasure; good-bye*
THISTLE	*retaliation, harshness*
TULIP	*declaration of love*
VIOLET	*faithfulness*
YARROW	*good health; cure for heartache*
ZINNIA	*thoughts of friends*

There is something simple about a cool color palette. Breezy and flowing, it captures the colors of the sky and fluidity of water at the same time.

True blue may be the color with the fewest options in the flower world as it frequently appears to be more periwinkle or purple. But a trip to the garden center presents an array of blue selections: delphiniums, hydrangeas, blue birds, and bachelor's buttons. Lavenders and purples, of course, are easily available in flowers such as tulips, lilacs, and even the treasured sterling rose. Designing a blue-based arrangement in truly blue pottery will emphasize the tones. But don't rule out the use of delicate pinks and rich burgundies in a cool palette. The softness of pastels is light and easy on the eyes, while deeper burgundies are dramatic and defining.

landscape designs

✻ **MATERIALS**
sheet moss
river rocks
7 stems of ajuga
5 stems of maidenhair fern
zinc tray

✻ **TOOLS**
garden scissors
floral foam

Floral displays need not be bunched, gathered, or mounded. This low and unobtrusive design is an escape for the senses. Equally charming, pieces such as this can easily be assembled with what you will find within no more than three steps from your back door. It is the perfect way to display lush ground covers and nature's mementos.

1 Slice the wet floral foam to line the bottom of the tray, adding a few higher spots to create a bit of topography. Cover the foam with moistened moss.

2 Create a few groupings of river rock, and scatter a few stones randomly, to create outcroppings.

3 Work the stems of the flowers and fern through the moss and into the foam, creating several small stands of growth.

container variation

The tone of this copper tray is the perfect complement to the warm shades of seashells. Scattered over a bed of sand, they are home to the new growth of small white flowers. The color combinations may be played with in great variation of tones. Both hardware and pet supply stores carry sand in myriad colors.

✳ **BOTANICAL MATERIALS**
chamomile
ladies' mantle

styling variation

This alternative style has the same premise, but it is colorful and lush. Vibrant tones of mixed phlox are displayed in a bed of sea glass, contained within the softer edges of a round green porcelain tray. The often-overlooked saucer element of the planter provides an unexpected design idea. Their colors are as ample in options as the pots they typically support. They are usually inexpensive, especially by mid- to late summer, when they can usually be purchased at significant discounts at pottery or garden centers.

summer delight

✳ MATERIALS
10 stems of asparagus
10 stems of lavender
white ramekin

✳ TOOLS
garden scissors
floral foam
sheet moss
wire bent into horseshoe-shaped pins about 1/2" (1 cm) long

A series of these arrangements across a mantel is simple and elegant. The lavender picks up the hints of lilac tones in the asparagus stems, while the white ramekin defines, without distracting, in a subtle and tasteful way. This crisp version would complement the sharp architectural details of a white Victorian mantel beautifully. A dark-stained wooden box instead of the ramekin would be more dramatic, making it the perfect complement to a mahogany-lined study.

1 Cut the wet floral foam to fill three-quarters of the ramekin. Cut the stems of asparagus to length, keeping the proportions of the container in mind.

2 Insert each stem of asparagus into the foam, grouping them in the center of the container. Add stems of lavender into the foam, throughout.

3 Fill the space around the arrangement with moistened moss, and use the wire pins to secure in place.

styling variation

Instead of being grouped in the center, the asparagus was cut shorter and used to rim the ramekin, extending the perceived height of the container. A mass of lisianthus blooms and buds fills the center, but garden roses or sweet peas would be just as lovely, especially in tones of blush pink or lavender, perfectly accenting the asparagus' colorings and textures.

✳ **BOTANICAL MATERIALS**
asparagus
lisianthus

color variation

Everything is warmed up with the fiery tones of this ramekin. The chestnut-colored fiddleheads' unique quality stands with beautiful form and grace. Peach hypericum berries perfectly complement the coloring of the container and assist the eye's transition from manmade to natural, softening the adjustment between the two extremes.

✳ **BOTANICAL MATERIALS**
fiddleheads
peach hypericum berries

: # soothing hues

✳ **MATERIALS**
12 stems of pale blue delphinium
5 stems of cream lisianthus
8 stems of maidenhair fern
blue sugar bowl

✳ **TOOLS**
garden scissors

Blue is an extraordinary color for flowers, and those that are available are stunning. Accentuate the blues by arranging the flowers in a similarly colored container, and set them off with a contrasting flower such as ivory lisianthus. White phlox or even geraniums would provide a similar effect, with florets similar to those of the delphinium.

1 Cut and arrange five of the stems of maidenhair fern in the sugar bowl, defining the size and shape of the arrangement.

2 Add the delphinium to further define the arrangement, giving it height and width.

3 To create fullness, tuck the lisianthus blooms between the delphiniums.

4 Use the lisianthus buds and remaining stems of maidenhair fern to fill in gaps and distribute visual interest.

container variation

The small tiles of this mosaic candleholder play off the fractured-light effect created by the dual tones of the delphinium. The variety of shapes in the container and of the flowers is visually exciting.

✽ **BOTANICAL MATERIALS**
pale blue delphinium
dark blue delphinium
dusty miller

color variation

Blue needn't be an icy tone. Here, the rich cobalt of the delphinium is enhanced by burgundy foliage, making the bouquet perfect for the hearty country-themed container. Clippings of the common garden annual coleus are used here, but depending on the season and your location, burning bush or red maple could be used with equal effect.

✽ **BOTANICAL MATERIALS**
dark blue delphinium
burgundy coleus foliage
fiddleheads

striking simplicity

✳ **MATERIALS**
3 stems of purple columbine
silver tussie mussie vase

✳ **TOOLS**
garden scissors

Columbines have a whimsical quality to them, all decked out in their jesterlike petals. Yet, the silver finish of the tussie mussie lends a refined touch to this ever-so-simple display. Experiment with mixing up the colors of the blooms, or try using a few stems of ranunculus instead, to achieve a chunkier yet still playful look. For a lush and abundant display, accent the rim of the vase with a tight cluster of freshly clipped garden roses.

1 Cut the stems of the columbines to varying lengths. In addition to the blooms, make use of the buds for added texture.

2 Arrange the blooms in the vase, allowing each to stand at a different height to develop a sense of depth and dimension.

styling variation

A white creamer has a farm-fresh feel, a look that is well-suited for flowers that can frequently be found by the side of a country lane. Take advantage of all the properties of the container, such as the pouring spout of this one. Note how the flowers flow toward the edge.

✳ **BOTANICAL MATERIALS**
columbine
green hypericum

color variation

The addition of peach roses adds a touch of sunny warmth to a cool backdrop of purple, green, and blue. Use pink pepperberries instead of the green hypericum to further enhance the richer tones, and move to a more vibrantly colored columbine in shades of red or yellow.

✳ **BOTANICAL MATERIALS**
peach roses
green hypericum
purple columbine

floral cuisine

Not only are flowers a visual feast, but many may tickle our taste buds as well. Several common blooms are just as wonderful served in the bowl as designed in it. Between roses, pansies, chamomile, nasturtiums, and sunflower buds, our palettes are whet with everything from savory to spicy to sweet. Candied pea flowers and daylily pancakes are just a couple of the recipes you could tackle. There is a wealth of information available, and cookbooks abound that are devoted to the subject. Remember: always make sure you know what you're eating and where it came from. Wash it thoroughly and don't consume florist shop flowers or anything picked from the roadside. Organic is always best. Even better choices are those tasty little numbers grown to perfection in our own garden beds.

CLOCKWISE FROM TOP:

lilac, pansies, chamomile, lavender, calendula

Herbs are a garden staple, but the blooms that blossom on plants such as oregano and basil are often overlooked as design elements. Purple basil and silvery sage add both unusual coloring and scent to a bouquet, and pairing them with the peppery fragrance of flowers such as freesia, rosemary, or chives creates a particularly stunning combination. As with flowers, if herbs are to be part of a visual and culinary delight, always make sure you know their origins and are aware of their chemical histories.

CLOCKWISE FROM TOP:

purple basil, sage, green basil, oregano, scallions, rosemary, parsley

green with ease

* **MATERIALS**
  3 stems of viburnum
  5 stems of tweedia
  3 purple anemones
  hosta
  lamb's ear
  dark glazed pottery

* **TOOLS**
  floral foam
  waterproof tape
  branch clippers
  garden scissors
  moss

Chartreuse flowers, cool-tone hostas, and silvery lamb's ear serve as a backdrop to tiny touches of color. Tweedia adds star points of periwinkle that are perfectly juxtaposed to the larger shapes of the bouquet. Tweedia is generally only available from your florist, but when the season is right, adorable Johnny-jump-ups or forget-me-nots found outside serve as more than suitable substitutes.

1 Prepare the container with the floral foam, floral tape, and moss.

2 Create the shape of the bouquet as you add the stems of viburnum. Fill in the design with the hosta and lamb's ear.

3 Snip the tweedia stems to length, and add them to the arrangement to bring in a touch of color. Add a bolder punch of color with the inclusion of the anemone blooms.

✳ texture variation

A hand-thrown piece of pottery displays a busier selection of botanical elements, while offering a very similar color scheme. All the shapes are quite small and feathery, keeping the eye in constant motion as it looks for a focal point to settle on.

✳ **BOTANICAL MATERIALS**
tweedia
freesia
maidenhair fern
lamb's ear
green hypericum
ajuga

✳ color variation

In this arrangement, hydrangea is the flower that brings in the spring green tone. In striking contrast, rich pinks enliven an otherwise cool palette, but the design could easily be mellowed with soft blush pink or soft peach tones instead.

✳ **BOTANICAL MATERIALS**
green hydrangea
thistle
roses
phlox
geranium greens

hens and chicks

* **MATERIALS**
  4 hens and chicks
  7 chocolate cosmos
  4 sprigs of stonecrop
  moss
  bird's nest basket

* **TOOLS**
  wire
  garden scissors
  stem tape
  plastic bag
  hot-glue gun
  floral foam
  waterproof tape

Hens and chicks are a low-growing ground cover used in backyards and garden beds. There is a certain quality to its coloring that makes it appear as if the light is always shining on it, yet it is sublimely cool and subtle. Even with the touches of burgundy around the edges—played up in this arrangement with the addition of the chocolate cosmos—the arrangement remains calm and collected.

1 Line the basket with the plastic so that it will hold the water. Hot-glue the plastic to the rim of the basket and trim with the scissors. Fill with the water-saturated floral foam, and tape it in place.

2 Wire the hens and chicks using two pieces of wire inserted perpendicularly to one another through the stem. Fold the pieces together and wrap them with stem tape to create a stem about 3" (8 cm) long.

3 Insert the hens and chicks into the foam to define the shape of the arrangement. Make sure the actual base of the green is pushed into the foam. Tuck in bits of moss to hide the foam.

4 Add the stonecrop and chocolate cosmos.

styling variation

In contrast to the very informal, tongue-in-cheek approach to the first design, this variation is pure elegance. The ivory crackled pottery on a weathered copper base elevates the styling to a different echelon, in tandem with a new, but still cool-tone, palette of accent flowers.

✳ **BOTANICAL MATERIALS**
hens and chicks
night-blooming jessamin
purple sweet pea

styling variation

A wondrous woodland path is re-created in this small arrangement. Rising high above the hens and chicks are shoots of wild indigo and Solomon's seal. Ferns, princess pines, or hostas could also be used with equal success. Design inspirations to create this piece will be plentiful on your everyday walks.

✳ **BOTANICAL MATERIALS**
hens and chicks
wild indigo
Solomon's seal

purple playland

* **MATERIALS**
  3 alliums
  3 scabiosas
  white jug

* **TOOLS**
  garden scissors

Alliums announce fun without saying a word. Their shape is so playful and carefree that thoughts of childhood games and stories immediately come to mind. Recollections of children's gardens shared with butterflies resurface to be rejoiced in. This simple arrangement lets the very structure of the flowers speak for them, proving the adage "less is more" to be true.

1 Cut the alliums to three different lengths; height variation will maintain a sense of movement and activity.

2 Place the alliums in the jug, paying attention to which direction the stems bend for the most visually pleasing placement.

3 Fill in around the alliums with the scabiosa, using it to both echo and complement the primary flower.

styling variation

While the overall structure of the allium is unique, the fullness of the bloom makes it very useful for other design applications. Here, the stems are cut very short so that only the purple flower is used, defining a lush, tight shape for the other design elements. Phlox (used here), hydrangea, geraniums, and agapanthus all offer a similar structure and proportion, and pair well with the allium.

✳ **BOTANICAL MATERIALS**
allium
white phlox

color variation

Purple may be a cool-tone color, but it blends beautifully with warmer tones. Both the roses and the red toile pot offer a stunning contrast to the allium's hue. Mix it up with lilacs to mimic the plushness of the alliums, but with a more elongated shape that breaches the mounded frame.

✳ **BOTANICAL MATERIALS**
allium
peach roses
orange spray roses

plum crazy

* **MATERIALS**
  2 plums
  3 bunches of green grapes
  2 kiwis
  2 vines of ivy
  cylindrical glass vase

* **TOOLS**
  garden scissors
  water tubes

Fruits make a wonderful addition to arrangements, but they also can become a beautiful arrangement on their own. By allowing the design to begin at the bottom of the vase, the glass becomes a frame, perfectly containing the botanical painting.

1 Layer and stack the kiwis, plums, and grapes in the vase, maintaining space between the fruits and the container.

2 Sprinkle the blueberries over the other fruits, allowing them to trickle through the spaces to the bottom, and also to collect in small piles in other areas.

3 Insert the ivy into the water tubes, and then slip them into the arrangement, using the other elements to hide the tubes from view.

✳ botanical variation

The same color palette can be achieved with vegetables for a heartier presentation. Eggplants and green beans, accented with some roadside cuttings, make a cool offering, as well. Small red potatoes and tufts of chives could serve as additional embellishment.

✳ **BOTANICAL MATERIALS**
   eggplant
   green beans
   dock
   tule pod
   candytuft

✳ color variation

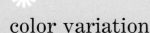

The assortment of glass vases available is impressive. Chunky glass is clean and modern in feel; cut and filigreed pieces add daintiness. Shop around to find the perfect option to offset your design ideas. You'll find ample selections at flea markets, yard sales, houseware stores, and craft and garden centers.

✳ **BOTANICAL MATERIALS**
   daisies
   tree clippings
   brussels sprouts

mellow burgundy

* **MATERIALS**
  2 stems lavender spray roses
  1 stem of Dordogne
  blue and white teacup

* **TOOLS**
  floral foam
  garden scissors
  moss

Deep red and burgundy tones can be cooled off significantly when paired with the chilliest of companions: silver-tone lavenders, as here, or navy blues. The color combination is unusual and striking, suited for winter soirées or autumnal gatherings. Depending on the season's offerings, you could tuck in a Bosc pear or kiwi for an earth-tone accent.

1 Prepare the teacup with the floral foam and moss.

2 Cut snippets from the Dordogne and use them to outline the shape of the piece. Add the blooms of the spray rose.

3 Use additional trimmings of the Dordogne to fill in and finish the arrangement.

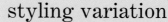

styling variation

Focusing on larger shapes creates a weightier bouquet. It is texturally less busy, yet visually just as interesting. The lavender keeps everything quite cool, and the unripened raspberries are just starting to warm to join the tones of the burgundy roses.

✳ **BOTANICAL MATERIALS**
lavender spray roses
burgundy spray roses
tree clippings
wild raspberries

botanical variation

A variety of flowers can be used to achieve this color combination, in the process offering different styling options. Purples and lavenders can be either cool in blue tones, or significantly warmer in red tones. Play with the combinations to find the perfect effect.

✳ **BOTANICAL MATERIALS**
lavender delphinium
astrangia

table settings

The centerpiece isn't the be-all or end-all of table decorating. Often times, with larger gatherings, there is so much happening on the table that it's hard to find room to set the arrangement. Fortunately, there are smaller touches, with equal impact, that bring individuality and grace to your table settings.

 tip Use a water tube for delicate or wilt-prone flowers, such as sweet peas and clematis, with a folded napkin. Slipped inside the fold, the tube will be perfectly hidden.

Bring the decorating to each place setting, and everyone will feel like a guest of honor. Slip something as elementary as a single leaf or a full bloom into a flat fold napkin. For a fuller look, bustle a napkin with ribbon to secure a hardy bloom.

Rather than trying to claim center space, line a few small dipping trays or saucers across the table, each floating a single bloom. Whether they contain identical flowers or several different varieties, nothing could be simpler.

Framing each plate with a vine such as ivy creates a truly decadent ambience. Experiment with the look: A ring around the plate is the perfect tailored cuff; or let the ends of the vines trail off the table to invoke visions of an enchanted forest.

Warm tones comfort us, romance us. Soft dusty rose, peach, and russet evoke late summer sunsets and autumnal fireside visions. They soften the edges of expectations and mellow us into relaxing with their coziness. A leonidas rose from the flower shop, combined with a golden apple and an orange parrot tulip snipped from the yard, warms the heart and soul.

The combination of tones available to create this comfortable ambiance is wide, varied, and sometimes surprising. The otherwise cool of grey-tinged lavender warms when coupled with rich burgundies. Navy hydrangeas exceed expectations when presented with Bosc pears and dusty roses. It is all richness: Decadence and opulence show softly yet distinctly with these hues. Experiment with and enjoy the treasure of warm and welcoming bouquets that deck the front halls and foyers and delight fast friends.

garden beds

✳ **MATERIALS**
10 tulips
sprigs of spurge
cream rectangular container

✳ **TOOLS**
garden scissors
floral foam
waterproof tape
moss

Keep it clean and simple by mimicking how the flowers grow. Designs like this make it appear as if you've dug up a small patch of garden. This arrangement adds the perfect touch of color to a windowsill or mantel. Multiple arrangements could line a stairway or hall to create an indoor garden path, or they could beautifully define and embellish the aisle of an outdoor wedding ceremony.

1 Prepare the container with the floral foam, waterproof tape, and moss, making sure it's level with the top of the container.

2 Add one stem of tulips at a time, cutting the stems to slightly different heights. Create some small groupings, and stagger the flowers slightly so they do not form a straight line.

3 Tuck small sprigs of ladies' mantle into the moss around the base of the arrangement, keeping a natural look.

styling variation

Play with shapes and form by using a round container instead of a rectangular one. Poppies and tulips present a delightful stand of elegance for the dining or coffee table. However, always keep in mind, particularly with dining table arrangements, that you and your guests must be able to see over the arrangement. Keep practicality in mind when considering all your design dimensions.

✳ **BOTANICAL MATERIALS**
   tulips
   poppies
   peach hypericum

container variation

A series of copper pots creates a progression of three individual groupings of flowers. Keep it simple by using flowers of the same family, or mix it up from piece to piece for a more varied look and a sense of surprise.

✳ **BOTANICAL MATERIALS**
   assorted daffodils

floral sunset

MATERIALS
10 dahlias
6 phlox
yellow string beans
gold schefflera
vintage white compote
small bowl

TOOLS
garden scissors
floral foam
waterproof tape
moss
wire

Warm summer nights are brought to mind with this arrangement of dahlias and beans that could have just been snipped out of your grandmother's garden. The vintage serving piece used as the container only enhances the effect. When working with an openwork piece such as this, line the interior with moss to hide the mechanics. Place a small bowl to hold the floral foam and water in the center. Prepare the bowl with the foam and water as instructed in Getting Started.

1 Use the schefflera to define the shape of the bouquet and add the dahlias.

2 Make small bundles of beans by wrapping them with wire. Keep the wire ends long so that you can twist them together to insert the beans into the foam.

3 Finish by adding the phlox, making sure the wire supporting the beans is hidden.

styling variation

Dahlias are beautiful when grouped lushly together, but one stem can have an equal impact. Here, a modern vase filled with assorted wax beans lends color and support to a single bloom. Dried beans could also be used for an earthy effect. Sea glass and marbles could be added as a mosaic foundation.

✳ **BOTANICAL MATERIALS**
   yellow and green beans
   burgundy dahlia

color variation

Burgundy dahlias and the golden-brown tone of Bosc pears create a rich, masculine mood. Dark ivy leaves frame the bouquet perfectly against a deep-colored urn. When working with such deep, rich tones, it is important to keep a bit of color variation and contrast in mind. Including these shadings prevents the bouquet from becoming too dark and lost.

✳ **BOTANICAL MATERIALS**
   burgundy dahlias
   Bosc pears
   ivy

sunken treasure

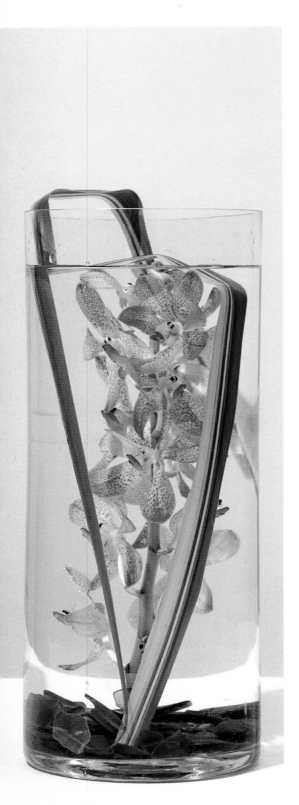

※ **MATERIALS**
1 stem dendrobium orchid
1 calathea leaf
glass cylinder vase
green sea glass

※ **TOOLS**
garden scissors
waterproof tape
wire
stem tape

A bloom under water is instantly magnified and takes on a certain magical quality. The impact of just one or two elements is impressive. These types of arrangements are mesmerizing when set ablaze by the sunlight or a ring of softly burning candles for an evening affair. Include candles that float across the surface, or pillar candles that break through and rise above the water.

1 Start with a clean, dry vase. Any moisture in the vase will prevent the tape from adhering properly.

2 Cut the orchid stem to about three-quarters of the height of the vase. Hook the wire over the last bloom, and use the stem tape to wire a 1 1/2" (4 cm) extension. Bend it back to form an L shape, and tape the stem to the bottom of the vase.

3 Layer the sea glass in the bottom of the vase to hide the tape, and tuck the calathea leaf around the inside of the vase. Slowly fill the vase with water.

color variation

The regal purple tones of these irises create a path for the eye to travel that starts at the bottom of the vase and continues to arc up and out of the vessel. Black pussy willow provides the perfect dramatic accent, but any decorative grass could substitute with equal drama.

✳ **BOTANICAL MATERIALS**
 iris
 black pussy willow

styling variation

Experiment with extending the arrangement beyond the water line and confines of the vase. Pulling elements from the watery backdrop into the space around the container creates visual interest and activity that dominates the setting and captures the eye.

✳ **BOTANICAL MATERIALS**
 dahlia
 lily
 thistle
 curly willow

garden harvest

* MATERIALS

3 burgundy snapdragons
3 red yarrow
coleus stems
oregano stems
cherry tomatoes on the vine
yellow pot

* TOOLS

garden scissors
wire
stem tape
waterproof tape

The backyard garden offers sustenance and beauty. Accented by a few flowers, edible treasures can be transformed into a tempting display of abundance. Experiment with different color schemes and textures to find the right combination for your home and palate.

1 Prepare the pot with a grid of waterproof tape (see "Preparing Your Containers," page 16). Use the coleus and oregano stems to define the shape of the arrangements and to hide the tape.

2 If the tomato vine is too short to use in the arrangement, wire it to lengthen its stem and add it to the arrangement. Allow it to drape over the side of the pot.

3 Add the snapdragons and fill in with the red yarrow.

color variation

The fiery tones of the tomatoes and peppers contrast beautifully against the cool tones of the flower accents in this simple, country piece. Alternatively, the color palette could be reversed using eggplants or grapes for the purple tones and bright nasturtiums, calendulas, or day lilies for a burst of color.

✳ **BOTANICAL MATERIALS**
   red and yellow tomatoes
   chili peppers
   rosemary
   hosta
   grape hyacinth

styling variation

The focal point of the first piece has now become this version's anchor. Submerged yellow tomatoes on the vine support a bundle of garden flowers, while the glass vase contributes a modern look.

✳ **BOTANICAL MATERIALS**
   yellow tomatoes
   cream sweet pea
   lavender
   coleus

heart of fire

* **MATERIALS**
9 stems of eremuras
7 stems of bleeding heart
1 hydrangea
green pottery

* **TOOLS**
garden scissors

This fiery display gets its support from the hydrangea head, rather than from a gridded top or floral foam. The practical beauty of this oversized blossom is that, when cut short to just fill the top of the pot, it provides ample structure for even the tall blooms.

1 Cut the stem of the hydrangea so that the head sits snuggly at the top of the pot. If it wobbles or seems a bit unbalanced, trim it a bit shorter.

2 Add the eremuras by slipping the stems through the hydrangea florets. Keep the stems in the center of the piece taller than those on the sides.

3 Fill in the arrangement with the bleeding heart making use of its inherent sense of flow and movement to finalize the fiery creation.

color variation

Everything has softened here, but the design still relies on the strong form of the eremuras. Paired with iris and lilac, this version is elegant and soothing. It's very cool in contrast to the original bouquet, offering hints of neutral color.

✳ **BOTANICAL MATERIALS**
white eremuras
bearded iris
lilac

styling variation

This piece is sculpture. It is all about form, color, and placement. The lentils echo the hue of the flowers and provide support. Add the flowers to the lentil base as soon as the water has been added. The legumes will absorb the liquid quickly, further securing the stems.

✳ **BOTANICAL MATERIALS**
red lentils
eremuras
lepto blooms

WARM-TONE   shades of harvest

* **MATERIALS**
  2 golden apples
  2 Dordogne
  3 crocosmia
  crackle-finish vase

* **TOOLS**
  branch clippers
  garden scissors
  floral foam
  moss
  wooden picks

Varieties of apples are numerous: golden, Granny Smith, lady, crab. Each has a distinctive quality to offer in size, shape, or shading. A supply of particular varieties ebbs and flows with the seasons, but this oldest fruit is always present.

1   Prepare the vase with floral foam and moss. Use the wooden sticks to insert the apples into the foam.

2   Add the Dordogne to provide width and height to the arrangement and to fill in around the apples.

3   Add the stems of crocosmia, making use of the bud stems, as well. This adds a touch of extra texture and furthers the sense of abundance.

container variation

Baskets are a plentiful resource; many offer a reflection of our locales. Certainly, a variety of local shops carry a multitude of different options, but yard sales and flea market are a wonderful resource, too. The baskets found in these places are aged and patinaed with character. This petite Nantucket basket perfectly cradles a botanical concoction rich and varied in textures and tones.

✳ **BOTANICAL MATERIALS**
golden apple
rose
viburnum berries
dock
yarrow
millet grass

botanical variation

The vibrant red of the crocosmia is paired differently here for a fiery effect that is busy with movement. With no large elements to anchor the eye, it is perpetual motion of petals and leaves. The combination of brilliant color and haphazard shape tells an exciting story to pique our interest.

✳ **BOTANICAL MATERIALS**
crocosmia
hair allium

WARM-TONE sun worship

* **MATERIALS**
  8 coreopsis
  dock
  red pottery

* **TOOLS**
  garden scissors
  waterproof tape
  floral foam
  moss

The sun itself is mirrored on the faces of these darling little flowers. Gathered into a topiary shape, they become a beacon of shining light. If you want to work on a larger scale, you can substitute sunflowers for the coreopsis. The heads of these majestic flowers truly trace the path of the sun.

1   Prepare the pottery with the floral foam. Tape it in place, keeping the center free from obstacles so the stems of the topiary can be inserted.

2   Working in your hand, gather the coreopsis into a topiary shape. Trim the stems to all the same length, and insert them into the center of the foam.

3   Add the dock to decorate the trunk of the design. Cover the base with moss to hide the mechanics.

color variation

Daisies and sunflowers blossom in countless shades of summery yellows, but they also promise autumn with suggestions of umber, rust, and chocolate. Choose the mood that you are trying to achieve and consider the container you are using to create the perfect color combination and pairing of tone and form.

✳ **BOTANICAL MATERIALS**
rudbeckia

styling variation

The design, the chosen container, and the botanical companion of the primary elements are all variables that influence the finished bouquet. Despite the informality of the coreopsis, the whole design is refined by its pairing with peonies and the elegance of the pottery.

✳ **BOTANICAL MATERIALS**
coreopsis
black-eyed Susan
blush peonies
tree clippings

wild berries

* **MATERIALS**
  3 roses
  3 green berry trimmings
  5 raspberry trimmings
  zinc pot

* **TOOLS**
  garden clippers
  garden scissors
  floral foam
  moss

The roadside hosts innumerable treasures, but favorites by far are wild raspberries, blackberries, and blueberries. There are also endless varieties of wild berries that inspire design even though their names have been long lost. Make use of them; their beauty is unlimited.

1 Prepare your container with the floral foam and moss. Clump the roses together in the foam to start the shape of the design.

2 Add clippings of the green berries to further define the lines of the arrangement and accent the roses.

3 The raspberries both enhance the color of these roses and put the finishing touches on the bouquet. Add the stems to fill in any empty areas in the arrangement.

botanical variation

The raspberries work just as beautifully with more formal flowers that display a tone similar to that of the roses. Keep in mind how colors complement each other as you try working with plants such as privet or pepperberries. Understanding the shadings that are reflected and enhanced by neighboring elements is an important skill in mastering the subtle coloring of your designs.

※ **BOTANICAL MATERIALS**
  peonies
  cymbidium orchids
  wild raspberries

styling variation

This bouquet is focused on the berries, with the floral element taking a back seat by mimicking the size and shape of the tiny fruit. The intricacies of shape and color are further echoed in the beading of the container, creating an array of intricate details to keep the eye and imagination in motion.

※ **BOTANICAL MATERIALS**
  wild raspberries
  green berry clippings
  purple ageratum

peaches and cream

＊ MATERIALS
4 white monkshoods
2 cream roses
3 orange roses
3 stems of peach hypericum berries
viburnum greens
white urn pottery

＊ TOOLS
garden scissors
floral foam
waterproof tape
moss

This is the loveliest and softest of color combinations, elegant but not overdone. As the name suggests, this palette would be well-suited for the inclusion of some fresh peaches, apricots, or nectarines tucked beneath the foliage or nestled beyond the berries. Other ideas are limited only by the season's harvest and your imagination.

1 Prepare the pottery urn with the floral foam, tape, and moss. Add the stems of monkshood, varying their heights slightly, and defining the vertical lines of the piece.

2 Tuck the roses in to give body to the base of the arrangement, but still allowing for some depth and dimension.

3 Use the berries and greens to fill in the shape and size of the bouquet.

styling variation

While the monkshood gave height to the previous piece, the diminutive proportions and the plumpness of the roses pull this bouquet into a tighter, lusher shape. Good use is made of a common household item: a frosted votive glass.

✳ **BOTANICAL MATERIALS**
orange rose
cream rose
peach hypericum

color variation

Rosy tones warm the presentation with the addition of garden astilbe and rose variations. Eliminate the cream shadings altogether for an even cozier setting. As the color scheme deepens, the bouquet becomes more engaging.

✳ **BOTANICAL MATERIALS**
white monkshood
dusty pink roses
orange roses
cream roses
pink astilbe
peach hypericum berries
viburnum greens

follow the leader

✳ **MATERIALS**
2 stems of peach Calibrachoa
  hybrid
horsehair-embellished vase

✳ **TOOLS**
garden scissors

Common garden annuals, available at garden centers, grocery stores, and farm stands, are a delightful, but often overlooked source for cuttings. These stems of peach Calibrachoa were chosen to echo and highlight the etchings on this neutral vase. The container you work with can offer inspiration for your flower design—even something as simple as mimicking colors, tones, or shapes.

1 Select cuttings that best duplicate the shapes and forms presented by the vase.

2 Cut the stems to the appropriate lengths and arrange them in the vase, keeping the overall visual in mind. Don't allow the piece to become too cluttered.

container variation

The glistening beads of this candleholder are dramatically reproduced in the jewel tones of the flowers and greens, which have a certain translucent quality of their own. The beauty of flowers that have this quality is that they always seem to be sunlit. This is also true of bi-tone blooms or flowers that have inherent natural shadings.

✳ **BOTANICAL MATERIALS**
cymbidium orchid
spurge
yarrow
hair allium

container variation

An unusual basket is the cornerstone of this striking, architecturally appealing display. It is all about space and, in some ways, what's not there rather than what is. The eye follows the lines and shadows created by the ethereal reachings of earthly elements.

✳ **BOTANICAL MATERIALS**
oregano flowers
wild grasses

✳ weddings

Weddings are the perfect opportunity to express individuality, whether you prefer country charm or modern simplicity. Flowers are not the focal point for the day, but the arrangements and bouquets chosen will certainly add beauty and style to the couple's perfect union.

A beautiful altar piece is English garden styling at its best. Delphiniums, roses, and viburnum offer a warm and elegant palette, while still portraying friendly comforts. Small-town churches and country chapels frequently delight in neutral simplicity, providing the perfect backdrop for a color scheme of your choice. If the walls, stained glass, and other details of the interior architecture are deep and multifaceted, however, choose the more neutral tones of the wedding palette for the altar bouquets to ensure their visibility.

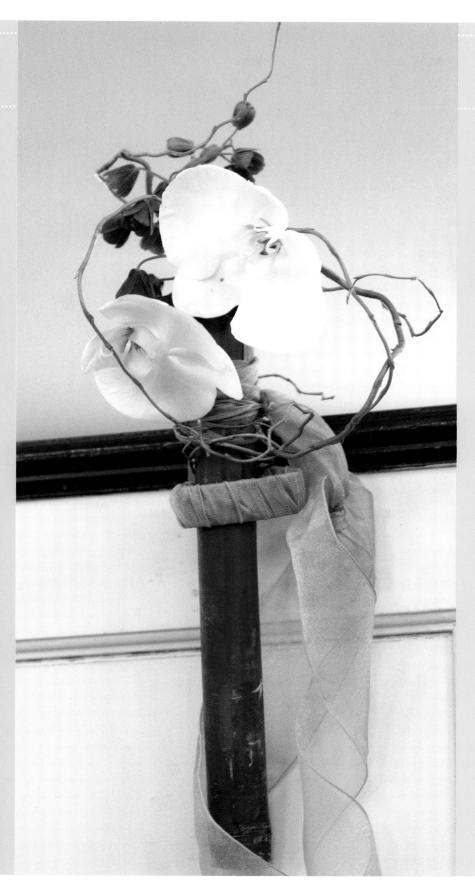

Adorning the aisle may well be the most important decorating done at a ceremony site. It sets the stage and draws the audience in by marking the ceremonial path. A simple phalenopsis orchid stem, fritillaria, and a few branches lay the groundwork for calm serenity.

MONOTONE RECIPES

The visual simplicity of monotone palettes is an oasis of calm in the midst of busy lives. The designs may be tailored and modern with a geometrically formed style, or may offer the contrast of loosely arranged country quaintness.

Single color bouquets excel in a variety of settings. Against a busy backdrop of kitchen clutter or a room designed in prints, the piece becomes a focal point and escape from visual chaos. It gives the eye a place to settle. For a space that is monochromatic, a similarly toned grouping of flowers delights with a subtle hush of nature. Or pull the design in another direction by introducing a posh yellow touch to a singly red room.

With the quiet of the colorings, texture moves to the forefront. Delicate florets of lily of the valley are distinct against a full white peony, but bloom after bloom of purple bearded iris offers simplicity of form that echoes the uniformity of tone.

solo act

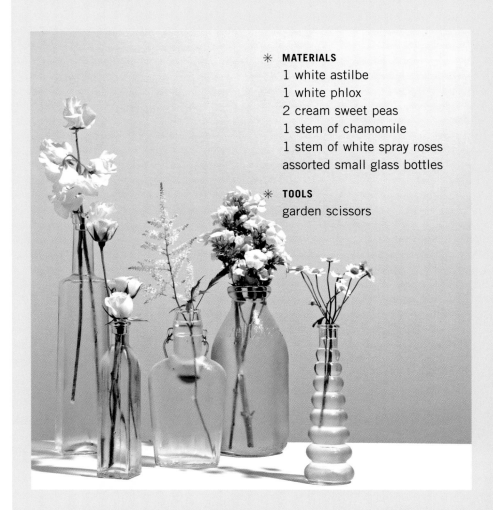

✳ **MATERIALS**
1 white astilbe
1 white phlox
2 cream sweet peas
1 stem of chamomile
1 stem of white spray roses
assorted small glass bottles

✳ **TOOLS**
garden scissors

Beautiful design is sometimes so easy that it seems we must have forgotten something. This charming combination keeps a simple color tone interesting with a variety of shapes and textures in both the flowers and the bottles used. A small grouping like this is precious on an end table or lined up in a row along a narrow windowsill.

1 Select a grouping of bottles that vary in height and width to create the most visual interest.

2 Place each flower in the bottle that proportionally best suits it. The delicate chamomile should be tucked into a smaller bottle, while the larger phlox is best suited for a chunkier selection, such as a milk jug.

3 Arrange the bottles into a grouping, placing the larger ones in the back and the shorter ones in the front.

styling variation

A collection of vintage soda bottles lined in a row make a kitschy work of art from the simplest of designs. The beautiful soft yellow blooms of the hyacinth, cut all to the same height, continue the uniformity. To add variation to the sight line, cut two stems taller than the others.

✴ **BOTANICAL MATERIALS**
yellow hyacinth

container variation

This includes a similar assortment of flowers as the first design, but the jewel-tone glasses bring in a shot of color. This is monotone with a kick—perfect for enhancing the limited colors of flowers you may have found in the woods or in your garden.

✴ **BOTANICAL MATERIALS**
white phlox
white astilbe

purity

* **MATERIALS**
9 white lily blooms
6 stems of astilbe
pale blue pot

* **TOOLS**
floral foam
waterproof tape
moss
garden scissors

Lilies are one of the oldest flowers. Representing purity, they have been incorporated into our rituals since the beginning of time. Their inherent meaning and disarming fragrance are pleasant when they stand alone, but they are even better paired with a soft accent.

1 Prepare the container with the floral foam, tape, and moss.

2 Arrange the lily stems in the foam, keeping everything tight, allowing the shapes of the petals leaning up against one another to add textural interest.

3 Fill in with the stems of astilbe, allowing them to extend slightly beyond the lilies to add a sense of depth and dimension to the bouquet.

color variation

This bouquet uses the same concept of a primary flower that defines the shape with fullness and then an accent of something wispier, but the color is bumped up to striking intensity with the use of the magenta ranunculus. This flower also softens the piece because it is such a plump, round specimen in contrast to the lilies.

✳ **BOTANICAL MATERIALS**
ranunculus
pink veronica

container variation

A tall vase provides height for an otherwise low, plump bouquet, and the various elements give color contrast to the same set of textures as the other arrangements. Clematis, a climbing vine frequently found entwined around lampposts and mailboxes, acts as a strong focal point.

✳ **BOTANICAL MATERIALS**
viburnum
pink veronica
clematis

golden feast

✳ **MATERIALS**
   4 yellow roses
   6 apricots
   wild greens
   lemon-print tin container

✳ **TOOLS**
   floral foam
   waterproof tape
   moss
   branch clippers
   wooden picks

The taste of the apricots is almost on your lips, as your eyes feast on this enticing arrangement. Combining garden and farm stand finds with greens picked from the random bush that rims the backyard creates a simple and appetizing delight. The inclusion of fruits or vegetables in a bouquet is always an enhancement.

1 Prepare the tin with the moss and floral foam. If your container is not watertight, first line it with plastic, as necessary. Add the greens to define the shape of the piece.

2 Use the wooden picks to arrange the apricots, nestling them in and around the greens. Placing the fruit next to a sturdy stem of greens adds an extra source of support.

3 Add the roses, keeping them roughly at the same level as the apricots, to create fullness and density.

color variation

Cut flowering crab apple branches from the tree at the end of the drive and combine their creamy whiteness with the warmth of yellow roses. The blue on the pottery offers further contrast with the roses, while the white coordinates with the apple blossoms. A vase of an entirely different color could prove a daring contrast and superb backdrop for this bouquet's simple color scheme.

✳ **BOTANICAL MATERIALS**
  yellow roses
  crab apple blossoms

styling variation

The decadence of summer fruits is nestled tightly in the base of this arrangement, but the calendula breaks loose, freeing up the design. Calendula is the perfect accent, being an edible bloom on its own. The color combination perfectly reflects the pattern of the pottery, without duplicating it.

✳ **BOTANICAL MATERIALS**
  kiwi
  strawberry
  calendula
  crab apple blossoms

white on white

✳ **MATERIALS**
8 white peonies
7 lysimachia
2 hosta leaves
silver basket

✳ **TOOLS**
garden scissors

This beautiful bouquet has everything to offer. Formal yet simple, this assortment of blossoms is lush, but wild at the same time. The lysimachia adds movement to a design anchored by the density of the peonies. Wild sweet peas or lupines would make perfect substitutes to keep the arrangement in motion.

1 Fill the basket with water and add the peonies, keeping everything low and lush. Use some of the smaller peony heads to add a bit of height difference from the rest.

2 Add the lysimachia stems, scattering them throughout the piece. Be sure to take advantage of their natural bends and curves.

3 Slip in the two hosta leaves as a finishing touch.

styling variation

The plump peonies are front and center in this piece, and they are further enhanced by the contrasting robin's-egg blue of the creamer pitcher. Kitchen containers may well provide the greatest inspiration and versatility. Open the cupboards and look around. Sugar bowls and flour tins, even old jelly jars, can take on a new purpose.

✳ **BOTANICAL MATERIALS**
white peonies
pink peonies

color variation

The striking contrast between the viburnum and the raspberry-toned peonies is an exotic combination. Mosaic glass tiles in the vase evoke Mediterranean qualities that ignite the imagination to travel to far-away places filled with heavenly scents and balmy breezes.

✳ **BOTANICAL MATERIALS**
dark pink peonies
viburnum

savory delicacies

* **MATERIALS**
dill
rosemary
dusty miller
oregano
scented geranium
aged terra cotta pot

* **TOOLS**
garden scissors
floral foam
waterproof tape
moss

The variety of green tones that Mother Nature provides us with is endless. Everything from the silver tones of dusty miller, artemesia, and lamb's ear to the deepest forest greens of oregano and cedar is waiting to be picked and added to gathering baskets. The strong scents of these mixed garden herbs provide another sensory delight, teasing the palate with savory adventures to come.

1 Prepare the terra cotta pot with the floral foam, floral tape, and moss. If you are using a garden pot with a drainage hole, line the container with plastic before filling it with the foam.

2 Start the arrangement by first adding the larger elements, such as the scented geranium leaves and dill heads, to define the shape.

3 Finish by filling in the design with the rosemary, oregano, and dusty miller.

color variation

Herbs need not be evocative of a country setting. Arranged in a silver julep cup, a striking bouquet is created that is polished with refined and natural elegance. This one includes the sweetly scented lavender, which colorfully plays off the silver.

✳ **BOTANICAL MATERIALS**
   dusty miller
   scented geranium
   dill
   oregano
   lavender
   lamb's ear

styling variation

Sage and garden roses are a traditional Swedish mix. Experiment with the colors of both the roses and the sage, which is available in purple or silvery green tones. Or for added drama, substitute red basil or purple sweet potato vine for the sage.

✳ **BOTANICAL MATERIALS**
   garden roses
   sage

crimson lady

✳ **MATERIALS**
24 mixed red roses
1 dark pink rose
multi-tone red glass vase

✳ **TOOLS**
garden scissors
pipe cleaner

Roses are available in a wide spectrum of reds. To ensure that your bouquet does not become too dark and that the flowers maintain their definition from one another, work with several different shades of red.

1 Arrange in your hand one stem of red roses at a time, working outward in a circle until there is a tightly tailored, domed bouquet.

2 Tuck in the one pink rose for a surprising touch of color. Tie off the bouquet with the pipe cleaner.

3 Clip the stems to an appropriate length for the container, and place the bouquet in the vase.

textural variation

A vintage green glass flea
market find is the perfect vessel
for an arrangement of burgundy
ranunculus and red hypericum
berries. The assorted small
shapes and the looseness of
the styling add texture while
maintaining the overall palette.

❋ **BOTANICAL MATERIALS**
burgundy ranunculus
red hypericum

palette variation

Deep colors are intense and beautiful,
but can sometimes get lost in the
shadows. Very pale tones may be
paired with darker ones, but allow
for a progression of shades that
keep the bouquet from appearing
too much like a polka-dot design.
This arrangement blends the color
range from ivory, to cream, to peach,
and then to red, by using a mix of
roses, lisianthus, poppies, and gold
schefflera.

❋ **BOTANICAL MATERIALS**
burgundy ranunculus
peach and red roses
poppies
lisianthus
gold schefflera

white magic

✳ **MATERIALS**
10 white anemones
green apple

✳ **TOOLS**
knife
garden scissors
wire

Smaller arrangements like this are perfect accents for individual place settings at a family dinner or friendly gathering. The container created by the hollowed out apple allows purely botanical elements to stand alone, without distraction. An arrangement like this can be assembled with ease, but given the limited area available to hold water, it should be done immediately before its presentation. If you need to make it a bit in advance, core the apple and brush it with lemon juice to keep it from browning. Keep the whole arrangement in the refrigerator until needed.

1 Arrange the stems of anemone in your hand, adding one at a time, to create a plump, lush shape. Tie off the bouquet with a piece of wire and set it aside.

2 Hollow out the apple as if you were carving a pumpkin, keeping the bottom intact to hold the water.

3 Cut the stems of the anemones short and tuck the arrangement into the apple.

color variation

This color combination is dramatically different, offering rich, somber tones, while using very similar elements. When you change the color or type of fruit you are using, a new inspiration will present itself. Work with the season's heartiest offerings, and your table displays will fit the feast at hand.

✳ **BOTANICAL MATERIALS**
   red apple
   burgundy coleus foliage
   purple pansies
   violas

container variation

Subtle neutral tones echo each other, providing a sense of highlights and shadows, in a design of camel and Sahara roses with brown eggs. The foliage of the ivy vines frames everything to perfection against this squash vase. Monochromatic extremes could be easily achieved by using a butternut squash as the vase, instead.

✳ **BOTANICAL MATERIALS**
   roses
   brown eggs
   ivy
   squash

MONOTONE : **tiling**

* **MATERIALS**
  8 stems of peach yarrow
  green baking square
  sand

* **TOOLS**
  garden scissors

The simplest of concepts can often yield magnificent results. This square of yarrow evokes a mossy carpeting effect that stands well on its own or could be grouped with others of the same design, creating a geometric assortment of several varieties that tile the table top. Vary the size and shapes of the trays and you'll have a patchwork display that defies the traditional view of the centerpiece.

1 Fill the bottom of the baking square with a layer of sand. This will hold the flowers in place. Add water to a level just below the top of the container.

2 Cut the heads of the yarrow into very short pieces, just long enough to reach over the top of the baking tray.

3 Insert the yarrow clippings into the sand, filling the entire container. Allow for a little bit of height variation for a mossy look. Keep everything exactly the same height for a more uniformly tiled appearance.

color variation

Here, striations of color are created by using several different shades of yarrow. When working with color, be sure to use intermediate values of your darkest and lightest colors to create a blended look. Too stark a contrast between the tones can make everything appear disjointed.

✳ **BOTANICAL MATERIALS**
yarrow

botanical variation

A stylish vintage plant tray found at a yard sale is the perfect setting for a modern presentation of this design concept. Stripes of various plant materials combine textural and shading variation. For a more formal feel, create each stripe of color with roses or hydrangea.

✳ **BOTANICAL MATERIALS**
reindeer moss
sheet moss
spurge

design idea

Be daring. Centerpieces invite creativity as they are the work of art the guests' eyes will be on most of the evening. An arrangement designed to look like sushi adds a touch of whimsy to a fun-loving atmosphere. These small floral bites are each made from bundled flowers wrapped tightly with a leaf.

vines of drama

* **MATERIALS**
5 vines of purple clematis
white chandelier with taper
candles

* **TOOLS**
garden scissors
hot-glue gun

Candlelight suppers are more
romantic with delicate tendrils
of vines softly brushing the
table. Early summer clematis,
cut from the trellis just outside
the back door, is enchanting—
summer breezes are the only
things missing from the indoor
garden that has been created.

1 When pairing plant
materials with the
presence of open flames,
make sure that the
candles are securely fixed
to the chandelier.

2 There is no water source
for the elements of this
design, so clip and arrange
the vines immediately
before they are needed.

3 Tuck or intertwine the
vines around the
chandelier. When needed,
use a dot of hot glue to
secure in place.

color variation

For an ultra-feminine styling, combine the daintiness of the white and crystal chandelier with long stems of pale pink flowers. For the most dramatic presentation, let the vines hang low so that they almost brush the tabletop. A tamer styling would dictate keeping all the botanical elements closely cropped to the container.

✳ **BOTANICAL MATERIALS**
fuchsia

styling variation

The darker tones of the chandelier, paired with the unusual flowers and ivy vines, create a much more masculine appeal. Set on a sturdy wood table, this design easily warms the night for candlelit dining or quiet study in the den. Using some of the votive holders as vases, this presentation promises long-lasting blooms.

✳ **BOTANICAL MATERIALS**
agapanthus
ivy

MONOTONE | # pink perfection

* **MATERIALS**
2 stems of candytuft
pink bud vase

* **TOOLS**
garden scissors

Monotone is more evident when you work the vase or container into the color scheme, as well. Even if the container can only hold a few stems, the effect can be mesmerizing. This arrangement could be duplicated with substitutes of wild sweet peas, geraniums, or flowering oregano. An additional design element is interwoven into the effect with the translucency of the glass. The subtle shadowing of the encapsulated stems adds a touch of intrigue.

1 In a container with such a narrow opening as this one, make sure the vase is filled with enough water. Given the limited space, it is likely that some stems will be cut fairly short.

2 Arrange the stems, starting by filling out the bouquet around the neck of the vessel.

3 Add the remaining blooms, building on what has already been done, slowly increasing the height of the overall design.

color variation

Rings of blue and white are echoed with the subtle shadings of the flowers, supported by the narrow neck of this bud vase. Delicate nigellas are used here, but a plumper variation could include blue and white variegated hydrangeas in the center ring.

✳ **BOTANICAL MATERIALS**
nigellas

botanical variation

Rather than working with the color, use the plant material to extend the lines and augment the shape of the vase. This clear glass enables the design to start at the bottom, intertwining the branches in a shape to mimic the vase shape. Once the clippings break the surface tension, nothing holds back the profusion of leaves that finish off the shape.

✳ **BOTANICAL MATERIALS**
tree clippings

festive wreaths

Wreaths are a popular holiday decorating technique. They are staples of many annual festivities. Frequently overlooked, however, is the abundance of alternative shapes and styles to be used at the designer's discretion when you go beyond the norm. There are endless combinations of textures, colors, and shapes that can be combined to make wreaths that complement your tastes and decor.

Valentine's Day, or any day noted to celebrate life's loves, is typically geared toward feminine delights. To augment the typical offerings of chocolates or flowers, this handsome rosemary wreath is a perfect masculine charmer. The design is simple, with a savory, not flowery scent. Mimicking his necktie, a chocolate grosgrain ribbon stretches the design. And everything must not be perfectly upright. Make it fun by hanging the wreath at a jaunty, fun-loving angle.

The Christmas holidays need not be all
evergreens and pinecones, adorned with
thick velvet ribbons that are difficult to work
with. Everything should be simple, especially
amidst the stresses of the "giving" season.
Sprigs of viburnum berries and their auburn-
tinted foliage offer enduring and natural
elegance without complication.

Celebrate the festivity of winter with a gathering of its representational charms. Bundled twigs and branches form a sturdy outcropping of support for snowy white lysimachia. Tufts of grass offer a representational twist on the enduring evergreen, reminding us of the promise of spring, and new life, still to come.

design idea

Typically, wreaths are formed from wired fresh or dried flowers and greens. A living wreath, however, is a self-sustaining alternative. Work with a sturdy frame to give support to soils and mosses, and plant your wreath with small ferns, ground covers, and ivies for a display that outlasts every holiday.

bibliography

Barash, Cathy Wilkinson. *Edible Flowers: From Garden to Palate.*
Colorado: Fulcrum Publishing: 1993.

"Common to Botanical Names." July 2004.
www.plantideas.com/names/common1.html

"Index of Plants by Botanical Names." July 2004.
www.botany.com/index1.html

"Flowers by Latin Names." July 2004.
www.zaplana.net/flowers/asp/flower_all_en.asp

"Floriography: The Language of Flowers." July 2004.
www.tlt.com/phpweb/index.php?module=article&view=8

"Language of Flowers." July 2004.
www.victorianbazaar.com/meanings.html

"The Language of Flowers." July 2004.
www.earthlypursuits.com/FlwrsPer/FlwrName.htm

Mandleberg, Hilary. *Dried Flowers.*
New York: Watson-Guptill Publications: 1999.

Packham, Jo.
Wedding Flowers: Choosing and Making Beautiful Bouquets and Arrangements.
New York: Sterling Publishing Co., Inc.: 1993.

Plants Database. July 2004.
www.plantsdatabase.com

Pritchard, Tom and Billy Jarecki.
Madderlake's Trade Secrets: Finding and Arranging Flowers Naturally.
New York: Clarkson Publishers: 1994.

Wall, Carly.
Flower Secrets Revealed: Using Flowers to Heal, Beautify, and Energize Your Life.
Virginia: A.R.E. Press: 1993.

resources

Inspiration surrounds us, and it usually makes its appearance when we stop looking for it. But the travels, shopping sprees, and adventures that nudge our creative juices are what drive our artistic pursuits. Your local phone books and Internet directories will likely point you to numerous vendors, gardening centers, and craft supply stores. Your daily papers and the fluorescent poster board signs on the corner telephone poles will point you towards the best yard and rummage sales in your neighborhood. Keep your eyes open, and the flowers, potteries, and tools needed for the success of your flower design endeavors will certainly reveal themselves.

NATIONAL SUPPLIERS

Afloral.com
PO Box 526
Celoron, NY 14720
(888) 299-4100
www.afloral.com
Dedicated to floral supplies, tools, and materials

Ben Franklin
(800) 992-9307
www.benfranklinstores.com
Floral and craft supplies, containers, and baskets

Crate and Barrel
(800) 967-6696
www.crateandbarrel.com
A wonderful source for bowls, vases, pitchers, and other elegant and unusual containers

Fiskars
(800) 500-4849
www.fiskars.com
A wide range of scissors, clippers, and gardening shears; also available internationally

FloraCraft
1 Longfellow Place
PO Box 400
Ludington, MI 49431
(616) 845-5127
www.floracraft.com
Floral and craft supplies, baskets, and containers

Home Depot
2455 Paces Ferry Road
Atlanta, GA 30339
(800) 553-3199
www.homedepot.com
Containers, sand, pebbles, and garden tools

Jo-Ann Fabric and Craft
841 Apollo Street, Suite 350
El Segundo, CA 90245
(888) 739-4120
www.joann.com
Floral and craft supplies, containers, and baskets

Lowe's Home Improvement Warehouse
P.O. Box 1111
North Wilkesboro, NC 28656
(800) 445-6937
www.lowes.com
Containers, sand, pebbles, and garden tools

Michael's Stores Inc.
8000 Bent Branch Drive
Irving, TX 75063
(800) 642-4235
www.michaels.com
Floral and craft supplies and containers

Pier 1 Imports
301 Commerce Street, Suite 600
Fort Worth, TX 76102
(800) 245-4595
www.pier1.com
An extensive source for bowls, vases, pitchers, and other elegant and unusual containers

Target
1000 Nicollet Mall
Minneapolis, MN 55403
(888) 440-0680
www.target.com
A wonderful source for bowls, vases, pitchers, and other elegant and unusual containers, also clippers, shears, and other gardening tools

INTERNATIONAL RESOURCES

Bravura Florist Supplies
Unit 7, Technology Rd.
Birch Copse Business Park
Cabot Lane, Poole, BH17 7FH,
United Kingdom
01202 659555
www.bravurafloristsupplies.co.uk

Creative World
The Bishop Centre
Bath Rd, Maidenhead, SL6 8ES,
United Kingdom
01628 665422
www.creativeworld.co.uk
Art, craft, and gift superstore with a natural and floral department

Fusion Flowers Magazine
Hillcroft, Fore Rd.
Kippen, FK8 3DT, Stirlingshire,
Scotland
01786 870957
enquiries@fusionflowers.com
www.fusionflowers.com

Laine's Floral Art and Hobby Crafts
60 Commerce Street
Insch, Aberdeenshire,
Scotland AB52 6JB
01464 820335
www.lainesworld.co.uk
Extensive craft and floral supplies; ships internationally

NAFAS
National Association of Flower
Arrangement Societies
www.nafas.org.uk
Flower arranging organizations
www.theflowerarrangermagazine.co.uk
Magazine for flower arrangers and floral designers

Smitcraft
Unit 1, Eastern Road
Aldershot, Hampshire GU12 4TE
United Kingdom
01252 342626
www.smitcraft.com
A wide array of craft and floral supplies

CUT YOUR OWN FLOWERS

Wildflower Farm
10195 Highway 12 West
Coldwater, Ontario LOK 1E0
Canada
(866) 476-9453
www.wildflowerfarm.com

Ashbank Farm
11440 John Marshall Highway
Markham, VA 22643
(540) 364-0436
www.ashbankfarm.com

Belvedere Farm
2840 Pleasantville Road
Fallston, MD 21047
(410) 877-1927
www.belvederefarm.com

Island Flower Farm
367 U.S. Route 2
Grand Isle, VT 05458
(802) 372-8867
www.islandflowerfarm.com

Wet Rock Gardens
2877 North 19th Street
Springfield, OR 97477
(541) 746-4444
www.wetrock.com

FLEA MARKETS

www.Sable.co.uk/fleamarkets/cities.asp
Locate flea markets across Europe.

www.fleamarketguide.com
State-by-state listing of local markets in the United States

www.discoverfrance.net
Listings of France's best flea markets

www.darcity.nt.gov.au/markets/markets.htm
A small selection of some of Australia's best-loved markets

© Tara Wrobel

about the author

Jessica Wrobel began her professional life as a costumer and paper and fiber artist, retailing her handcrafts in boutiques throughout New England and teaching art to the students of the ARC of Haverhill, Massachusetts, and Second Step/YMCA of Lawrence, Massachusetts.

She was able to explore further the rich world of decorative techniques when she authored *The Paper Jewelry Book* and *The Crafter's Recipe Book* (Rockport Publishers, 1998).

A love of natural materials and a series of coincidences drew her into the field of floral design twelve years ago, leading to the establishment of Jwrobel, a floral design studio, with an emphasis on special events. Her designs are regularly featured in such periodicals as *Elegant Weddings, Wedding Style,* the *Boston Globe Wedding Magazine*, and the *Knot*. She has also appeared on *The Victory Garden* for WBGH, Boston.

acknowledgments

I have an abundance of gratitude for all those who have made this project a reality. Special thanks go to Mary Ann Hall and Betsy Gammons of Rockport Publishers. Thanks to Silke Braun for her artful and creative guidance in directing the photography for this book. John Cosner, of CosnerPhotgraphy.com, Tara Wrobel, and Allan Penn: thank you for the extraordinarily beautiful photography. Sincere thanks to Delilah Smittle of Rockport, Patrick Porter of Chester Brown Wholesale, and Peter Fraisenett of Cornell University's Bailey Horatorium for your professional expertise and research efforts. Priscilla Clark and Mary McCarthy, your mentoring has been a blessing. To my family and the friends who extend that family, there are too many of you to mention. I am honored by your presence. Thank you.